CW01373847

# Change isn't What You Find in Your Pocket

Effective Change Methods for Delivering Market-Leading Results

## Simon Costigan

Text Copyright © Simon Costigan 2022

Simon Costigan has asserted his right in accordance with the Copyright Designs and Patents Act 1988 to be identified as the author of this work.

All rights reserved.

No part of this publication may be lent, resold, hired out or reproduced in any form or by any means without prior written permission from the author and publisher. All rights reserved.

First published in 2022 in the UK

3P Publishing, C E C, London Road
Corby NN17 5EU

A catalogue number for this book is available from the British Library

ISBN: 978-1-913740-73-3

Cover design: James Mossop

This book is dedicated to my wife Louise who has provided me with the unwavering support, wise counsel and unconditional love that I've needed to complete my own change journeys.

Thank you!

# Contents

## Preface

- Where It All Began — 1

## Delivering Successful Change — 5

- What is change and why is it important? — 5
- Business Change: The Reasons Why — 7
- Another Fine Mess You've Got Me Into — 10
- Simple Steps for Approaching Successful Change — 16
- Master Stakeholder Engagement — 23
- Make It Stick — 30

## Strategy — 36

- Don't Just Sit There, Think of Something — 36
- Identify Tasks and Priorities — 39
- Time To Get Creative — 41
- It's How Long? — 45

## Leadership — 51

- Leading The Change — 51
- Emotional Intelligence Through Change — 56
- Leadership Pressure — 61

- A Wise Monk Once Told Me... 66
- Boost Your Thinking Time 72
- Sure-fire Ways to Engage Your People 77
- Guarantees To Make Your Meetings Better 81

**Cornerstones** 89

- Difference Between Change, Programme and Project Management 89
- The Secret to Successful Project Management 95
- Case Study – Project Sweetshop Boots UK 111

**Conclusion** 114

**Testimonials** 116

**Acknowledgements** 125

**About The Author** 127

# Preface

## Where It All Began

I remember vividly the time when I realised that I was unhappy at work and that I needed to change the direction of my career. There is a reason behind every change and mine was the need to find greater fulfilment and achievement than I was experiencing in my role. I knew I had to embark on a journey that would take me from corporate employee to owner of The Change Partner.

I was working long hours and two to three days a week in London. Sitting in front of my laptop at 10pm was a regular thing and frankly it was becoming unhealthy. The impact on my family was evident. I was tired, grumpy, and not great to be around. It was a case of "if I don't do it now I never will". Feeling the need to leave a business I'd been in for 28 years for an unknown future was daunting, but I was ready to embrace the change and challenge that came with it. Losing the corporate safety net and a regular salary was a scary thing at the time. Ultimately, if it didn't work out, I'd have to find a job somewhere else, and I was comfortable with that.

I'd always wanted to run my own business, but how?

I then saw an advert for a programme manager needed to support the delivery of a big retail merchandising project for a Nottingham-based retailer. My god, I thought, there's only one of those. To cut a long story short, I applied, and was successful in landing a role with Momentum Instore Ltd, a company specialising in merchandising solutions. I left my desk at Boots on Friday and then walked the length of the building to start another role, leading a small, external programme team delivering the largest merchandising programme in Europe that year, 2,500 shops, 26,000 individual modules and over a million individual parts in six months. I remember people asking me if I was a bit mental for wanting to do it; for me, it would either define or kill my career.

I was in a leadership role for the first time in a long time and I had an amazing team of people working for me. I agreed crystal-clear expectations with them, agreeing what the expected standards were. I then gave them 100% autonomy to deliver their role in a way they felt was best for them, whilst making sure they knew that whenever they needed me, I'd be available.

The result: we absolutely nailed it, on time and under budget! The amount I learnt in those 15 months working with some amazing people has been the highlight of my career to date.

At the end of August 2018, I walked off the Boots campus for what I knew would be the very last time. That leap of faith has put me in a position from where I can now share my experiences and what I've learnt both in those 28 years I had in one of the biggest companies in the world and in market leading organisations such as DFS, Wilko and Holland & Barrett. Having the opportunity to understand how different businesses work and how the leaders in those business conduct themselves has given me a huge appreciation of the fact that people should be at the heart of everything a business does.

The positive energy I now feel every morning and the complete control I have over what I do and who I choose to work with is what I value more than anything. I love what I do and the buzz I get from supporting a business or an individual is difficult to describe. I could say it's better than sex, but I'd be lying!

Whilst the book focusses primarily on delivering change in large businesses I do believe that the principles in the book can be also applied to a smaller business by concentrating on the fundamentals of delivering change initiatives. This would include, knowing your reason why, being clear on who your stakeholders are and having a clear plan that you can monitor to ensure you have achieved everything you set out.

The same is true for personal change where you would need a catalyst for the change. As an example, if you were looking to start a new exercise routine, you would need your reason why, your own internal motivation, a support network around you and a vision of what the future you looked and felt like.

I have on occasion and deliberately highlighted certain themes such as the importance of effectively engaging people and having a clearly defined plan. I believe these are integral to delivering successful change and if you delivered these fundamental principles, you'd go a long way to accomplishing what you've set out to.

I hope you find this book insightful and thought-provoking, and that it helps you through any personal or business change journey you choose to embark on.

**'And suddenly you just know it's time to start something new and trust the magic of beginnings.'**
**Author unknown**

# Delivering Successful Change

## What is change and why is it important?

The dictionary definition of change is to "make someone or something different, alter or modify. It can also be defined as replacing something with something else, especially, something of the same kind that is newer or better".

Change has been with us since the dawn of time and will continue to be part of our everyday lives until the day we die. Without change we wouldn't be living the lives we do today. Technology innovations, medicine, environmental and societal changes are the constant threads that support everything we do from the second we get up to the second we go to bed.

It also plays a huge part in popular culture - the likes of David Bowie, Sheryl Crow and Michael Jackson have all sung about it. Ginger Rogers, Elvis Presley, and Woody Harrelson have starred in films about it.

There have also been copious amounts of books written on the topic of change, copies of Switch by Chip and Dan Heath, The 7 Habits of Highly Effective People by Stephen R Covey and The Happiness Project by Gretchen Rubin have sold millions of copies as both individually and collectively as a family or a business we often seek to change our current reality into something that we believe will be better.

**As Heraclitus put it "change is the only constant"**

Personally, I feel that change is an opportunity to reflect, refresh and renew current circumstances moving from our present reality to a place where we can improve ourselves, our relationships, and our working lives whether you work for a company or run one yourself.

I believe change is important as it enhances our lives. As Covid-19 proved, if we're forced to change, we can do it quickly and effectively, from creating vaccines in record time or ensuring people can work from home on a global scale. We now have two constants that we didn't have previously and in the case of working from home on a more regular basis an argument can be made that our work/life balances have improved as a result and the global impact of travelling has reduced carbon emissions.

> *"Change is never a matter of ability, it's always a matter of motivation"*
> *Tony Robbins*

## Business Change: The Reasons Why

Change is all around us, from our new ways of working due to the uncertainty Covid-19 brought through to the latest technology innovation that's available to us with ever-increasing regularity. For us as individuals and as businesses, the importance of understanding what we want to achieve is crucial, so the first question you need to be asking yourself is: why do I want to make a change, either personally or professionally?

Thinking about instigating change can be a scary thing to do. It's going to take you out of your comfort zone and into a place that you may find difficult: a place where you need to challenge your thinking, resilience, and emotional intelligence.

The reason for change can range from being unhappy about your lifestyle through to a regulatory change that a business must make to be compliant with the latest legislation. Whatever the reason, it's important that you are clear in your reason why, as this will give you a greater understanding of what you want and what you don't.

I'll give you an example. In 2012, a friend of mine set up a bike ride across the Pyrenees in France to raise money for his charity Headcase, which was founded after his wife passed away due to a brain tumour. I trained for the event to a level that I felt would lead me to being successful. *How wrong I was!*

Four days into the ride I had to pull out due to injury, which ultimately was due to my lack of preparation. I was devastated, as I felt I'd let down the people who had sponsored me to complete the ride, Colin who had organised the ride and who was a very close friend and Becky who the ride was being done in memory of. It was incredibly important to me that I finished it and I'd failed. I removed myself from the group for a few hours to process what had happened and I'm not ashamed to say that I shed a few tears that afternoon sitting on a mountain side. The empty feeling, I experienced is something I will never forget. I've never been comfortable with not achieving what I set out to and as I sat reflecting, I made myself a promise that I'd be back and the next time I'd complete it.

So, in 2014 I started training again. My two key motivations were to prove to everyone including myself that I could complete the event and to ride over the iconic Tour de France mountains I'd missed. My first training session was on New Year's Day, I had a plan, I had the belief, and I had the focus and most importantly I had the support of the people around me who knew how much it meant to me. I trained solidly for nine months, and in September I rode the 710km from Biarritz on the west coast to Colliurre on the east coast, traversing 11 mountains and over 13,000m of ascent. It was one of the greatest experiences of my life and one I'll never forget. The camaraderie, the sense of togetherness, the highs and lows we shared is something

I have rarely experienced. Riding into the coastal town of Colliurre on a hot sunny day and dipping my toes in the Mediterranean whilst sipping champagne made the hours of training and dedication worthwhile. Having failed and then succeeded I now understand that you can do anything you set your mind to, it's just a matter of understanding what didn't work and making the necessary changes to achieve the outcome you want.

I believe we can all achieve the changes we want if our reason is compelling enough. If it's truly something we want to achieve, then we can make it happen.

*"In life, change is inevitable, in business, change is vital"*
***Warren G Bennis***

## Another Fine Mess You've Got Me Into

I've talked about the importance of change and how it's now a constant in our lives, and that by executing change well businesses and people can increase their effectiveness and performance.

But what if change isn't thought through properly and the consequences of making a change are done without a long-term strategy in place or a clear idea of the direction the organisation wants to take? What can happen?

We've all seen examples of this, from large global organisations through to football clubs; a decision has been made for the short term without the long term being properly considered. It's a classic case of moving away from an issue instead of moving towards an opportunity or misunderstanding what your customers want. Without a clear direction of what you want to change in your life or in your business, the impact will be frustrating and costly, and will often result in no new benefits being realised.

### Watford FC Relegation

Watford FC sacked Javi Gracia after four games of being in charge in the 2019/2020 season. He was sacked due to poor form in the league. Thirty minutes after he was sacked, former Watford Manager Quique Sánchez Flores was yet again appointed. He survived only until 1st December 2019. After getting only one win following his appointment in September, he too was fired. A caretaker manager was appointed for one game, before Nigel Pearson came in to manage the club. He led the Hornets out of the relegation zone and was sacked with two games to play. Hayden Mullins was appointed for the last two games of the season, losing both, resulting in them being relegated to the Championship.

For me, this is a classic case of not having a clear vision and direction for the club. Whilst football is now a multi-million-pound business, the people put in charge of the day-to-day management need to be given the time to implement their ideas and philosophy. Too much change at the top of an organisation can lead to instability, uncertainty, and a failure to deliver the desired results.

### McDonalds Innovation

McDonalds billion-dollar mistake started with a failure to understand the principles of flexible leadership. Simply put, the most effective leaders can juggle conflicting priorities and keep them in balance. They then quickly assess the consequences of each decision and how it might impact the organisation.

In McDonald's case, the leadership put too much emphasis on innovations that it failed to recognise how making changes to its food preparation would hinder its ability to maintain speed and keep costs down.

Believing customers wanted more customised orders, the head of the fast-food chain's US division overhauled the company's entire food preparation system to introduce a concept called "Made for You"

The initiative involved burgers cooked to order with freshly toasted buns. It required expensive equipment upgrades, and of course, it drastically slowed waiting times. Suddenly customers were waiting twice or three times as long to get something they used to pick up in a few minutes. Nevertheless, McDonald's leadership insisted on trying to make it work. Ultimately through, "Made for You" failed and faded into oblivion. It was an expensive mistake and one that damaged the company's stock price.

If McDonald's leadership had taken the time to collect feedback and tested the concept more thoroughly before rolling it out, it would have recognised that it misjudged what customers really wanted.

So given the dangers you can encounter, this is what needs to be in place to execute change successfully, so it delivers the benefits you intended:

1. **Clarity of future direction** – When change happens, it's vital to have this mapped out and to be clear what a good outcome would look like. It's also important to keep what has worked well previously. This will provide reassurance and reduce insecurity in the people experiencing the change. Have a plan of what will

happen when and when people can expect you to communicate with them; this will help reduce uncertainty.

2. **Engagement with the people affected by the change** – People are the greatest asset of any organisation and it's important to ensure they understand the change you want to make and the reason why. Having a team who believes in you and what you want to do makes your chances of success far greater. Very often, the group of people who are affected by the change have no idea why it's happening – and then we wonder why they become resistant, difficult, and obstructive to the change we want to make.

3. **A clear communication plan** – Communication needs to be the heartbeat of any change, with a plan that outlines what will be communicated, when it will happen, who will be the audience and why. As the saying goes, 'If you have nothing to communicate, communicate.' If people are unclear what's happening, they'll fill this vagueness with what they believe to be true.

4. **Leadership commitment** – The leaders in the business need to commit fully to the change, living and breathing it as part of their everyday working life. They need to deliver clear consistent messages to all people in the organisation to instill confidence and belief. As

the leader of the business, you're the person your people will look to in times of stress and uncertainty. The first conversation you must have is with your leadership team to understand how committed they are personally to supporting you deliver the desired change. You must all be aligned on how you plan to execute it and when you all leave the room there must be no dissension as this can quickly derail the plan. If people find that just one member of your team relates a different message this can instantly form a belief that the change won't happen as their boss isn't bought in.

5. **A clear plan to deliver the change** – As the saying goes, 'The devil is in the detail'. When implementing change, it's important to have a plan detailing the key milestones and when they'll be achieved. This will ensure that people can be held accountable for the part of the plan they have committed to deliver. The lack of a clearly defined plan will erode the confidence of all in the organisation, as the impression will be that it is disorganised and directionless. Once you have your plan, publicise it and keep people updated on your progress.

6. **Day-to-day line management** – Line managers play an essential role in ensuring any change is smoothly implemented. They are closest to the people who report to them, and they can provide an important link between senior leaders and colleagues. They can

provide a temperature check of how people are feeling, so plans can be put in place to ensure the change is implemented effectively. This should be done in group forums and in one-to-one conversations, if appropriate.

*"Nothing so undermines organisational change as the failure to think through the losses people face"*
***William Bridges***

# Simple Steps for Approaching Successful Change

Delivering change should be made as simple as possible. Below is a tried and tested approach that will deliver great results. The proven method I use is in two phases. Phase 1 is all about quick wins, what needs to be the focus to unlock opportunities that already exist in the business. Phase 2 is more about looking to the medium and long term, building a sustainable strategy for the business. This is about identifying where the market is heading in an industry and aligning the direction accordingly.

These are the 10 steps that I've used previously to unlock both short and long-term benefits.

### Example Approach

**Phase 1 – Immediate Wins**
- Confirm brief and expectations with the Senior Team
- Focus on understanding the business identifying immediate opportunities and potential risks
- Identify what's missing and what can be introduced to make a positive difference
- Unlock and action the immediate opportunities, minimising current risks
- Review progress against initial brief

**Phase 2 – Medium to Long Term Wins**
- Establish medium to long-term goals and objectives with the senior team
- Establish and agree a plan to achieve Medium to long term goals
- Implement agreed plan with clear goals and milestones
- Review progress against medium to long term goals
- Review people & leadership progress against agreed goal

# Immediate Wins

## Confirm brief and expectations with the senior team

Before any work starts, a clear brief on what will be delivered needs to be agreed with the senior leadership team. This will ensure there is no confusion or misaligned expectations between parties. In my experience a formal scope of work should be drafted, clearly capturing what will and, just as important, what won't be delivered. Having the objectives documented will serve as a central reference point, should anyone want to add additional work to the previously agreed scope.

## Focus on understanding the business, identifying immediate opportunities and potential risks

Once the scope of the work to be delivered has been agreed, it's important to understand the challenges facing you or your business, what opportunities are available, and what risks are prevalent and haven't been identified. It's also important at this point to get to know the key people you'll be working with; I've always done this through a series of one-to-one meetings. The key thing is to understand their frustrations and challenges and how you can support them to move their work forward with clarity. Always approach these conversations with an open mind, having no preconceived impressions of what you believe needs to be fixed. Your personal view could be very different from that of the senior people you're delivering the change on behalf of.

## Identify what's missing and can be introduced to make a positive difference

It's important to discuss with the senior team how effective they feel the processes, procedures and governance are, as this may provide some clues as to why performance isn't where it should be. Key questions to ask is: what are the challenges, the frustrations and vision for the future? This should be followed up with conversations with the people who use the processes and procedures daily to understand where they feel improvements can be made. The output of these conversations should be a clear action plan of what needs doing, by when and by whom.

## Unlock and action the immediate opportunities, minimising current risks

Now it's time to start to deliver on the action plan. This is best done through regular progress meetings that ensure the tension is held on what's been committed to. As I've already highlighted, it's important to deliver some quick wins to show people in the business that tangible change and progress is being made. One of the keys to success in this phase of the work is regular structured communication with all stakeholders.

## Review progress against initial brief

At the end of the first phase progress needs to be reviewed to ensure that the initial scope of work has been delivered. This should be done by way of a formal review with the business leadership team, at this time it's also a useful opportunity to start to discuss what the next phase of the work looks like and if not done so define a scope of work. This needs to be an open and honest conversation, as it's important to understand if any of the initial deliverables need to be continued. It's also helpful to review how the objectives from the first phase support the next phase of work.

## Medium To Long-Term Wins

### Establish medium to long-term goals and objectives with the senior team

Now the business has been stabilised and is functioning effectively, the attention of the work can be moved to the medium and long-term ambitions of the business. This is the time to start thinking about the future strategy. This should be based on existing and future market trends, where the growth opportunities are and what the leaders of the business feel is important from a people and business culture perspective. Again, these should be accurately documented in a scope document to ensure alignment between the person/business delivering the change and the senior leadership team.

## Establish and agree a plan to achieve medium to long-term goals

Once work on agreeing the strategy has started, there then needs to be an agreement on how long each initiative will take. As an example, if an organisational restructure is needed, how long, realistically, would that take? The secret to planning is to take your time and not rush. There is no point committing to do the restructure in three months when clearly it could take six or more. This plan should then be committed to and documented as a series of top-line milestones, I would recommend no more than ten. This long-range planning exercise should be looking at where the business wants to be in the next two to three years. How to achieve this is covered later in the book.

At this time, it's also helpful to review the organisation's leadership capability to understand if there are opportunities for improvement and what resources are available to support this.

## Implement agreed plan with clear goals and milestones

When you have the agreed scope of work and the key milestones clearly mapped, it's time to start to actively manage the work through a clearly defined meeting and governance structure. This should also include an agreed meeting and document structure to ensure that the agreed activity is delivered and people can be held to account for what they have agreed to do. Regular weekly and monthly meetings are essential to ensure the milestones are hit and the agreed scope of work is achieved.

### Review progress against medium to long-term goals

I would suggest that this is done on a quarterly basis to ensure that the original intent of the scope of work is being delivered to the agreed timescales. They should also serve as the opportunity to set the direction for the next phase of the programme, ensuring budget, resource and capability are all in place.

### Review people and leadership progress against agreed goal

I'm a firm believer that any processes or procedures are only as good as the leadership and behaviours that support them. Without it, I feel they aren't worth the paper they're written on. Actively reviewing the progress being made against the agreed leadership development plans is critical for the long-term success of the business. People are the lifeblood of any organisation and having leaders who are engaged and committed to delivering success through people is critical.

Having a clearly documented performance and development plan for all people in the organisation is very important as it'll help you identify who your rising stars are, those who are treading water and those who need to be managed closely due to under performance. I would recommend agreeing personal objectives at the beginning of the year, reviewing them on a quarterly basis. I did this when working for Boots UK and it proved very successful as the people who worked for me were always clear on the expectation. By reviewing objectives on a quarterly basis, you can also sign off any objectives that have been completed and add any new ones to ensure your people stay challenged and motivated. By having regular performance conversations, you can also avoid the awkward end of year conversation where you and the person working for you have a very different perspective on how they have performed over the last 12 months.

*"No matter how successful you are, change is always good"*
*Billy Beane*

## Master Stakeholder Engagement

I believe one of the biggest mistakes that people make when looking to implement business change is the lack of stakeholder engagement. Not enough initial thought and ongoing management is applied to such an important activity. I feel that stakeholder engagement should always be the first job for any change, programme, or project manager, because it sets the tone for how things need to be done.

## What is a stakeholder

The Oxford dictionary definition of a stakeholder is 'a person or company that is involved in a particular organisation, system, project etc, especially because they have money invested in it.'

For me this only scratches the surface of how important stakeholders are in dictating how successful your change agenda is. In my experience being close to your stakeholders and knowing what's important to them is crucial. I've always felt that building robust relationships with the key people I'll work with is one of the first things I should be focusing on, and I'd estimate that 50% of the time in any role I've done has been effectively managing them across all levels of a business. A misinformed or disengaged stakeholder can have a detrimental effect on what you want to deliver. I've seen a global cosmetics marketing execution change the week before launch because the Chief Marketing Officer hadn't been thoroughly engaged and therefore wasn't happy with the proposed execution. This resulted in frantic work and a lot of stressed people working day and night to get the new look and feel approved.

Below I explore six ways to master stakeholder engagement, which I believe will guarantee you success when working at all levels across a business.

### Understand who your stakeholders are

Before you have any conversations with stakeholders, first find out who they are. Think about everyone you'll encounter, from senior leaders through to the project team you may be leading. It's also important to understand the interest and influence of each of the stakeholders, so you can tailor your approach accordingly. I have used a four-box model like the one below to understand this at a high level. Think about who you'll be working with and map them by name and role in each of the boxes. Once this has been done, you should have an idea of who you need to speak to and when. Consider the influence that each stakeholder has and their level of interest. As an example, you would want to keep the senior leaders informed as they will be the key opinion formers and could have significant impact on the work being done and the project working group on a more regular basis, I would recommend that this is done fortnightly as a minimum.

Stakeholder Map - Who needs What

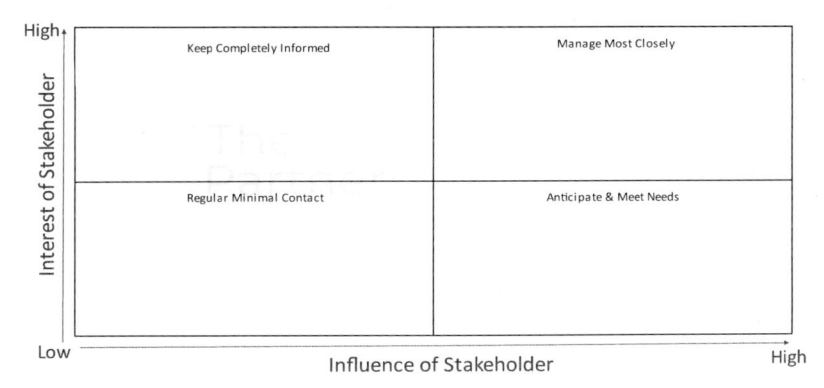

|  | Influence of Stakeholder → |  |
|---|---|---|
| **Interest of Stakeholder** (High ↑ / Low) | Keep Completely Informed | Manage Most Closely |
|  | Regular Minimal Contact | Anticipate & Meet Needs |

## Understand what is important to them

I've found the easiest way to understand what's important to a stakeholder is to ask them. Sitting down with them to understand exactly what they expect, also provides you with the opportunity to set your own expectations for the working relationship. What a radical concept!

Seriously, this is the easiest thing in the world to do, yet people don't take the time to do it. I can never understand why; maybe it's the fear of hearing another person's expectations clearly articulated. I feel that once you know the expectations, you're no longer guessing what that person wants and needs from you and as a result it's much easier to adapt your engagement strategy accordingly.

### Have a clear engagement plan

It's important to have a clear communication plan of who you'll speak to, how frequently and by what method. This will ensure that no stakeholders get missed as you lead the work. It should be checked on a weekly basis to ensure no one gets forgotten and everyone is properly engaged in the progress of the initiative. I have used plans such as the one below to great effect.

The stakeholder communication plan works in conjunction with the four-box model above. By having a plan like this, you can map out who you need to speak to, their role, their level of influence and their interest – you should capture this as high, medium, or low for both categories – what is important to them, how they want to be communicated with and how often, and any additional comments you feel are important for that stakeholder.

I used this plan when I led the global launch of No7's Lift and Luminate skincare serum for women. The senior brand manager and I mapped everyone we needed to speak to and how often. We then reviewed it on a weekly basis to ensure we'd been proactive in our engagement of all the key stakeholders especially the ones in senior positions.

This ensured they were all aligned with the progress, it also provided them with the opportunity to ask any questions they felt were important.

## Stakeholder Engagement Plan

| Stakeholder | Business Role | Influence/Interest | Key Interest & Issue | Communication Method | Frequency | Comments |
|---|---|---|---|---|---|---|
|  |  |  |  |  |  |  |
|  |  |  |  |  |  |  |
|  |  |  |  |  |  |  |
|  |  |  |  |  |  |  |
|  |  |  |  |  |  |  |
|  |  |  |  |  |  |  |
|  |  |  |  |  |  |  |
|  |  |  |  |  |  |  |
|  |  |  |  |  |  |  |
|  |  |  |  |  |  |  |

## **Take personal responsibility**

I've always felt that 50% of my job when delivering business change initiatives has been actively managing stakeholders. I always feel that if people are engaged and informed on the status of the work, the rest of the activity to deliver what's required is far easier. I've always found that an engaged stakeholder offers far less resistance than one who doesn't know what's going on. I believe it's your responsibility as the person leading to ensure this happens. You should be the glue that holds the whole thing together. I can't emphasise enough the importance of having the right conversations at the right time. I would recommend that you review your stakeholder engagement plan once a week to identify who you haven't spoken to recently, so you can proactively ensure that all your stakeholders are engaged and committed.

## Communicate, communicate, communicate

If in doubt, communicate, even if there is nothing to say, as this will give people confidence that you are still very much in tune with what's happening. Share quick wins that have been delivered; this is especially useful at the beginning, as it can help build momentum and people's confidence. Share personal success stories from around the teams; this will build a sense of community and possibly some healthy competition. I have found when communication isn't clear and consistent, people start to interpret things incorrectly and, in the absence of information, start to fill the void with what they believe to be true.

## Get to know your key stakeholders well

Take time to get to know your key stakeholders well. Seek to understand what's important to them outside of work as well as inside. I've always tried to do this and it's helpful when you are building a big relationship. It also helps that you have something to talk about other than work. Your key stakeholders should become your sounding board, your confidant and greatest supporter. Taking the time to cultivate these relationships will really pay dividends in the long run. I typically speak to all my key stakeholders on a weekly basis to keep it fresh and stay connected.

*'If you wish to persuade me you must think my thoughts, feel my feelings and speak my words.'*
*Cicero, Roman statesman*

## Make It Stick

One of the key aspects of delivering any change initiative is to understand how it will work in your 'business-as-usual' environment. Sadly, on many occasions this is something that organisations overlook, resulting in the benefits not being realised in full.

I've experienced both great and poor examples of this. When I implemented the Boots pharmacy at the Royal Hallamshire hospital in Sheffield we had a fully documented transition plan that was discussed and agreed with each of the departments affected as a consequence when it opened everyone knew how the service would work and what they were accountable for. Compare this with the programme I led for a leading high street retailer which was poorly executed due to the lack of people resources and budget that was allocated to the work. This resulted in large delays to the agreed timescales and therefore a postponement of when the agreed benefits realisation would be achieved.

Below are what I believe needs to be in place for you to nail the transition of your change initiative to 'business-as-usual'.

## Define how the project will work when part of business as usual

Before you start your change initiative, define how it will work when it's part of the everyday life of the business. To achieve this, I would encourage you to have a clear picture in your mind of what you want to implement, define what's in and out of scope and write it down. As an example, if you're introducing a new piece of IT equipment, does your Wi-Fi have the bandwidth to take the additional requirements? Let's be honest, it would be a disaster if your highly expensive new piece of tech didn't work because of a lack of bandwidth. Believe me, this does happen, and I've seen it in one of the businesses I've worked in.

Having your change clearly defined and scoped out will also give you a central reference point and will also prevent scope creep.

## Effectively engage the people affected by the change

As I highlighted previously before you start your change journey, ensure you have spoken to the people who will be affected to help them understand what's being delivered and why you feel it will benefit them. This could be a new piece of technology, an update to an existing process, or a governance process to facilitate better decision-making. If they aren't aligned and haven't bought into the change that you're looking to make they'll either not use it effectively or complain that their opinions weren't sought out, or they'll use it begrudgingly and then go back to the old process, as this is what they're comfortable with and believe in.

For instance, when I redefined the end-to-end process of dealing with customer complaints at DFS I used the people who were using it daily, this included the store administrators who received the complaint through to the service managers who would correct the issue in the customer's home. This ensured that when the new process was communicated and implemented across the rest of the business, I could highlight the fact that it had been done in consultation with their colleagues. This in turn gave the new process far more credibility and it greatly improved the adoption by others preforming the same roles. As a result, the number of complaints being received was halved in 12 months.

### Have a defined plan

To ensure you embed the change into your business, have a clearly documented plan of what will happen when. This should detail any training that needs to be delivered, dates of system switchover, if appropriate, and colleague engagement session both for those directly affected and those not. I would recommend that you co-create the plan with all the functional areas involved in delivering the business change. By doing this you get a greater level of engagement and accountability, as colleagues in the business have had the opportunity to articulate what they believe are the actions needed to be successful.

I would also recommend that you organise weekly cross-functional meetings to ensure your people are clear what they're accountable for and the key milestone dates that need to be achieved. Following these meetings, it's critical that you circulate the updated plan. This will enable people to see if any dates have moved, what the dependencies are and ultimately what they need to deliver.

**Prepare for the best, expect the worst**

What I mean by this is that even the best-laid plan can unravel, so have a plan in case you encounter problems when the transition phase starts. This can be achieved by conducting a 'what if' planning session. To make it a success, it's important that you have representation from every function affected. The idea of a 'what if' planning session is for people to capture everything they can think of that could conceivably go wrong and develop a plan for it.

As an example, when I led the self-selection cosmetics programme on behalf of Boots UK, one of the things we captured was the Chinese manufacturer falling behind on production, when this came to fruition, we had a plan to manage the issues, which was to increase the production in Poland while they caught up.

I would also suggest putting daily meetings in people's diaries for the first couple of weeks to manage any issues you may encounter; this enables the issues to be resolved quickly and efficiently. It's also easier to have the meetings in the diary and then cancel them than to have to try and schedule a meeting at the last minute if something goes wrong.

By doing this, I believe you can ensure that the people in your business will not lose faith in the change and what it means for the success of the organisation as you move forward.

### Make yourself available to your people

Embedding change in an organisation can be difficult due to the individual personalities involved. Everybody responds to change differently and it's important that you give people the opportunity to work through the change curve at their own pace; it's not something you can force or rush. The important thing as a leader is that you make yourself available to have conversations with your people, to ensure they feel listened to and that you understand how they're feeling and therefore do what's necessary to make their change journey easier. Your people are your biggest asset. Helping them navigate through the process will dramatically increase their performance and productivity.

I would suggest you speak with your people on a weekly basis both in any team meetings you have and on a one-to-one basis in case anyone has any specific concerns they want to discuss with you.

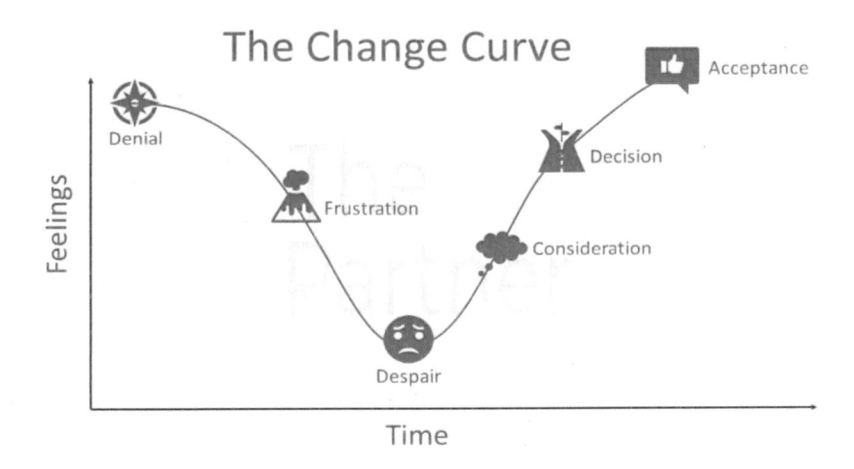

## The Change Curve

- Denial
- Frustration
- Despair
- Consideration
- Decision
- Acceptance

*Feelings* vs *Time*

**"Change is an event, but a transition is a process you go through in response to the change."**
**William Bridges**

# Strategy

## Don't Just Sit There, Think of Something

Businesses develop new strategies for many different reasons. These may include a global crisis, poor performance, evolving technology, new opportunities, reaction to internal and external pressure, mergers and acquisitions, and product and service changes.

When considering changing or developing a new business strategy, it should always be done from a place of moving towards an opportunity and not away from an issue. Let me explain further.

When we make decisions based on impulse or poorly thought-out concepts, typically through the fear of failure, there is the likelihood that the change in business strategy won't achieve the desired results. When considering making a change to your business strategy it's important that you take the necessary time to think through what the future direction needs to be, moving towards a new future and not fleeing the existing situation.

Typically, a full strategy review should set the direction of your business for the next two to three years. There should be a yearly review to monitor whether it still holds true or whether there are adjustments that need to be made due to changes caused by issues such as the Covid-19 pandemic. So how should you go about deciding what your business strategy needs to be? The following steps should be taken when formulating your strategy. **The key thing is start with the end in mind and work backwards.**

As an example, if you want to increase your customer base by 50% in the next five years, what do you need to consider, plan for and implement to make this goal a reality? Below are some things that you should take the time to reflect on when creating and reviewing your strategy:

1. Why do you want to change your strategy? What are the factors internal or external that are influencing it? Be clear about this and document it.

2. Define your goal and make it tangible. It's widely recognised that if you can visualise what success looks like it significantly increases your chance of success. You could use the SMART (specific, measurable, achievable, realistic and timebound) methodology to work through this. Ensure you address each of these thoroughly and, again, document it.

3. Think about how you would define success. As an example, I set myself 30 days to build and populate my website. This was my success statement:
*"To have The Change Partner website fully populated and launched by 4th June 2020 evidenced by a website that is being browsed by potential clients"*

4. Remember, you're the leader and your people will feed off your energy, either positive or negative, so consider what you are personally prepared to do to ensure success.

5. A significant barrier that may stand in the way of you successfully defining your strategy and your ability to achieve it will be your own mental blockers that limit your self-belief. Take time to reflect on these and what the triggers are; these could be past conversations and experiences. Just remember, the past doesn't predict the future. Consider who can support you to overcome these psychological hurdles that are impacting your personal effectiveness.

*"Strategy is not the consequence of planning, but the opposite: it's the starting point"*
*Henry Mintzberg*

## Identify Tasks and Priorities

Once you've decided on the goals that need to be included in the creation or review of your business strategy, it's time to start working out what activity you need to undertake to realise the objectives you've set for yourself. The most effective way of doing this is to give yourself and your team the permission to spend dedicated time working through exactly what you need to do to move your strategy forward.

Listed below are some suggestions on how you could approach this:

1. Brainstorm individually or as a team what you could possibly do to achieve the goals you have agreed. Nothing should be off limits, as people need to feel that they can think freely without fear of ridicule if they come up with an off-the-wall idea. You need to create a space for creativity. Challenge yourself and your team to come up with as many ideas as they can within an agreed time limit, I'd suggest no more than 10 minutes.

2. Once you have your list, prioritise your top five to seven tasks to focus on and to add more detail to. To do this, think about what resources are available to you; consider people, equipment, and anything else you feel would help you achieve your objective.

3. One of the biggest keys to your success will be identifying who can help you, who has expertise in subjects that you don't and who can you ask to collaborate and challenge you, so you get to a robust view of what you need to deliver.

4. Engagement and communication are critical in ensuring success. This will be either internally with the people that work for you or externally with the people whose help and support you need, or both. Share with them your clearly defined goals, explaining where they fit in and what you need from them. If you can do this effectively your chances of gaining buy-in increase significantly.

5. As you work through what you need to do, you'll undoubtedly encounter problems. To prevent risks becoming issues, it's important to consider what could knock you off track and stop you from achieving your goals. If you can identify and mitigate the risks you feel you'll come across, you increase your chances of success.

*"Strategy is a choice. Strategy means saying no to certain kinds of things"*
*Michael Porter*

## Time To Get Creative

So now it's time to get creative, stretch your thinking and be innovative. You're probably wondering what the hell I mean by that. The final piece of the puzzle is all about thinking outside the box and about what else you can possibly do to make the change you're about to embark on a complete success.

This could potentially be the most difficult part of working your way through the strategy you have defined for your business. This is because you must forget all your preconceived ideas and past experiences you carry with you, to think freely and without boundaries.

So how can you do this? Below are some ideas you should consider:

1. Think about some of the most successful people throughout history, not necessarily business. What have they done to deliver successful change? Think about Nelson Mandela, and how he went from being imprisoned on Robben Island to how he overcame apartheid; or Richard Branson, and how he went from his first business venture, a magazine called *Student*, to setting up Virgin Megastores in 1972 selling records to currently running over 400 companies.

2. If you close your eyes and envisage the future of your company after the change, what do you see, hear, feel?

What will the people who work in your organisation say about you and your business? Put yourself in their position; what would you want to have experienced?

3. Imagine you were a superhero; what would your special power be to bring successful change to your business? What would your name be? Let your mind wander and have some fun with it.

4. As touched on previously, you should also seriously consider doing 'what if' scenario planning (please refer to page 40, Prepare for the best, expect the worst). Think about every conceivable thing that could go wrong and have a plan for it. This should be a lengthy exercise if done properly, as you should leave no stone unturned. It would also be wise to involve the whole business in this exercise. This does two things: it gives people a sense of ownership and accountability, and it ensures that you haven't missed any key detail that could derail your plans.

5. Think about how you could do things quicker. This could be doing tasks concurrently, freeing up resources and time from around the business to focus on managing the change programme or initiative in its entirety. What could be the rocket fuel you need to accelerate the change in your business or personal performance?

6. How else could you access the information you need to deliver successful change? Think about blogs you

could read, YouTube videos you could watch that would help you understand what good looks like, and physical or audio books. There are countless opportunities to learn. It's your choice whether you decide to take them or not.

7. Consider making a public pledge to all the people in your business or sign up to a challenge that could support you with thinking through how to deliver the work you need to. Go MAD Thinking do a great 30-day challenge; it really gets you reflect on and explore what you need to think about and how to execute it. I made a public declaration on LinkedIn that I'd write the book that you're now reading. It's a powerful thing to do. Once you've put it out, there is no hiding place.

8. Decide on your first action. What do you need to do immediately to build some momentum or claim a quick win? Commit to a date to have it completed by, ideally in the first 24 to 48 hours. Get yourself into a place where you are clear about your intent and act upon it.

I believe it's also important to write down whatever you come up with, so you have a reference point to go back to. Having a document that has captured all your ideas is beneficial, as it enables you to reflect on what you can do to keep your strategy on track. A vision board placed in a location where everyone can see it is an effective and accessible way of achieving this.

*"Creativity is intelligence having fun"*
*Albert Einstein*

## It's How Long?

So, you've worked through your business change strategy, defining the goals, figuring out which tasks you need to do in what priority, and you've let your imagination run free to capture innovative solutions to ensure you deliver a compelling change plan for your business. It's now critical that you measure results as you work your way through the plan you have laid down. Outlined below are what I believe are the most effective ways to do this.

### Quick wins

To ensure you gain momentum quickly and to show people that you are fully committed to executing your change agenda, it's important to get a quick win under your belt. This could be as simple as following through on a promise you have made to the people in the business. It would also be a worthwhile exercise to look at your list of priorities to decide which you can do the quickest. Have the courage to circle a date on your calendar to have it done by and mobilise your leadership team behind it. Proving you do what you say you're going to do will increase the confidence of your people. As soon as you've achieved your first success, it's important you let everyone in the business know, as it will start to grow belief in your people that the change is achievable and that it's starting to happen.

An example of this is when I started working for Holland and Barrett, initially I was asked to lead a review of their process that ranged product in stores. When I started talking to people in the business it soon became apparent that the existing process wasn't joined up and didn't engage all the key people such as the Customer Insights team. As a result, there was a lack of understanding of what customers we're looking for, what the wider market forces were and what product innovation was market leading.

Within two days I had written a proposal that advocated making the process longer so that the insights team could conduct research into all the key customer metrics described above. By ensuring there was a clear view of what the customer was looking for in all the key Holland and Barrett categories such as Vitamins and Food we ensured that a compelling customer proposition was presented.

It also gave the business confidence that the larger piece of work that was required to look at the wider process and how it interacted with all the key functions was worthwhile and achievable.

### Governance and meetings

Depending on the size of your business, you'll need to consider the most appropriate way to manage the delivery of your change agenda. No matter how big or small, you should look to implement a governance and meeting structure to ensure risks, issues, dependencies, actions, and proposed changes can be handled effectively. I would recommend that this should include the decision-makers in your business, as well as the people who have been asked to bring the change to reality. As an example, the following roles could be included depending on the size of your business, the Chief Executive Officer (CEO), the Finance Director, the Head of Operations, the Programme Director, and the Programme Manager. There may also be a need to have functional representation to add greater value to the conversation.

The meeting structure could look like the hierarchy below.

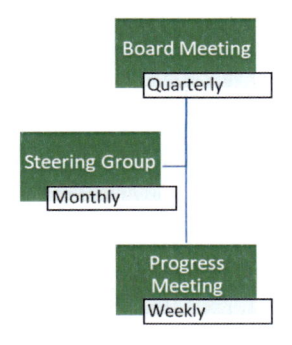

Board Meeting
Quarterly

Steering Group
Monthly

Progress Meeting
Weekly

Now let's explore what should be discussed in each forum to ensure the right conversations are being had to ensure you stay on track to realise the benefits you've identified in your strategy.

## Weekly progress meeting

The weekly progress meeting reviews the initiatives and projects sitting under your change umbrella. In these meetings, ensure you report by exception. What I mean by this is only talk about activity that is a risk or is off track; having conversations about activity that's on track doesn't add any value, so don't bother. The meeting should be used to review the plan you have agreed on, monitoring activity that's not tracking to the agreed timescales and agreeing solutions to course correct. You should agree on a set of actions to bring it back on track, when they need to be completed by and who's accountable for completing them. The meeting should also be used to monitor spend against the agreed budget. If the budget is at risk, a plan to bring costs back in line should be discussed. If no solution can be found, the issue needs escalating to the steering group for resolution. Finally, the meeting should also be used to review risks, dependencies, actions, and issues captured in previous meetings, closing, adjusting, and escalating as appropriate.

## Monthly steering group

As above, topics in the steering group should be discussed by exception and it should be purely used as a decision-making forum. If updates need providing on activity, these should be provided in any documents that are circulated prior to the meeting. The meeting should be used to advise on risks and issues that can't be solved in the weekly progress meeting. It should also be used to make decisions on any change requests and any deviations to budget. Finally, it should ensure that all current and future activity is tracking to agreed dates, providing guidance and solutions when they aren't.

### Quarterly board meeting

The board meeting should purely be a forum where senior leaders and shareholders are advised on the progress of the change programme. Only in exceptional circumstances when the steering group can't reach a decision should they provide the clarity that's needed to keep the change agenda moving forward. They should also agree on the budget and resources that are required to deliver the work, and as the work is done, they should be advised of how the spend is tracking against it.

### Documents and meeting etiquette

To ensure meetings are effective they should all be supported by the following documents:

1. An agenda that clearly states the start and finish time of the meeting, who's attending, what the discussion topics are and what decisions are required.

2. A risk, action, issue, and decision (RAID) log pre-populated with all the relevant information that is needed to keep the work on track. It should also detail who is accountable for

completing open actions and issues and what completion date has been agreed.

3. A milestone or detailed plan detailing all the relevant information that is needed to keep the work on track. This needs to capture the activity that needs to be completed, when it's due to start, the amount of time it's going to take, whether any other activity is dependent on the end date e.g., you shouldn't implement new technology into a business until it has been thoroughly user tested, who's accountable for completing it and finally whether the task is on or off track.

All documents should be circulated at least 48 hours prior to the meeting to ensure any that need reading by those attending can have opinions, questions and challenges formed on them.

Any actions captured in the meeting should be issued no later than the day after the meeting to ensure they can be started by the people they are assigned to.

*'Strategic thinking rarely happens spontaneously.'*
*Michael Porter*

# Leadership

## Leading The Change

Now more than ever, it feels like businesses are looking to change, to recover, survive or thrive in the ever-changing, fast-paced world that we live in.

As the leader, it's important that you have a clear idea of how you're going to navigate the organisation through the change to make it meaningful and sustainable. Ultimately, it's your accountability as the leader of the business or functional area to realise the change you're making and its associated benefits.

It's also important to lead by example and model the behaviours you expect from your people, everyone that works for your will eventually mirror the way you conduct yourself. As an example, I've worked for leaders who answer emails at unsociable hours, ultimately what ends up happening is colleagues feel compelled to do the same. So, if you believe in your people having a balance between their work and personal life, you must live to those values.

## Clearly articulate the reason why

As we have covered earlier in the book, and I can't stress this enough. All change must have a clearly defined reason why and how it supports the delivery of the business's wider strategy. It could come in the form of organisational, technological, process or cultural change. The one thing that is consistent through all of these is the need to take time to think about what you want to achieve and then to clearly articulate and document it. Having your reason why committed to paper will ensure a consistency in communication and alignment with the rest of your management team.

### Set clear, achievable objectives

Once you have defined your reason why, a set of clearly defined objectives should be captured. These will help people understand what needs to be delivered, by when, by who and how success will be measured. Sounds obvious, but unfortunately many businesses pay lip service, and as a result they fail to deliver on time, to standard or to budget.

### Manage your energy

As the leader of the business, you'll be the one people look to when they're feeling uncertain, worried, or resistant to the change that's happening around them. This can result in you expending a lot of personal energy. It's therefore important that you make time for yourself to recharge your batteries, so consider how you do this. It could be yoga or family time; whatever it is, make time for it. The better you feel, the better you'll be for your people.

### Celebrate success early

As you travel along your change journey, you will encounter people who have experienced failed change and will therefore remain unconvinced that you can successfully deliver the agreed objectives. Celebrating success early, no matter how small, will start to convince people that what's happening is working and worthwhile. If people can see that their colleagues are making progress and benefiting from the change you've instigated, it will smooth the path to quicker adoption in the rest of the business.

### Make yourself and your leadership team available

We all know about the emotional cycle of change and the peaks and throughs that people go through. What's sometimes less recognised is that people can go through it more than once and may also experience a sense of loss of a previous role or colleague who may have left. As the leader, it's important that you ensure both yourself and your leadership team are available to have supportive conversations to help people move through the change they are experiencing.

### Take the time to speak with your people

As I highlighted earlier, I believe you can't underestimate the power of communication when taking your people on a change journey, talking to them on a regular basis it vital.

Communicating too much is better than not enough. A failure to do it at regular intervals through various channels can lead to people making up the narrative for themselves with them needing to fill the communication vacuum. This can have a serious impact on how smoothly the change happens. People's individual perception can very soon become reality and once this is in place it can be very difficult to move people to a place where they fully understand the change that's happening and what it means for them. Have a written plan that details what will be said, by whom, when and by what channel, e.g., face to face, video, written, etc. It's important to keep your messaging consistent and aligned throughout your business to ensure people are clear on what's happening. Poorly thought-through or executed communication can lead to resistance, which could have been avoided.

## Party hard!

When you've delivered your change agenda, it's important to celebrate success at the end to recognise what people have experienced and how much you value how they have managed their personal change journey. For some people it may have been difficult and stressful, and as a leader it's crucial that this is recognised. I would suggest that you make everyone aware of the date and diarise it, so people have something to look forward to. You could also pay for the first round of drinks as a thank you. Let's be honest: no one needs an excuse to party!

*"Leadership deals with people and their dynamics, which are continually changing. The challenge of leadership is to create change and facilitate growth."*
*John C Maxwell*

## Emotional Intelligence Through Change

I passionately believe that people should be put at the heart of every change an organisation undertakes, and as a leader your level of emotional intelligence can have a critical influence on how you lead your people through it. Very often, processes, tasks and systems are prioritised over the emotional and mental wellbeing of our people, resulting in change that is painful for leaders and colleagues alike.

Over the years, I've delivered largescale change programmes, and firmly believe that the processes, tasks, and systems that a business has are only as good as the behaviours that underpin them.

I found this approach particularly beneficial when I started to engage the trading team at Holland and Barrett in the new process to range product instore.

Initially I presented the proposal at the monthly steering group to gain buy in from the three trading directors, this ensured that when I started to engage the people in their teams, I would meet less resistance. I also asked for a nomination from each of their teams that I could work with so the new process could be tested on their next range review and to get feedback on what worked and what didn't. This proved valuable as there were certain aspects of the new process, I hadn't considered such as where to get the source information from to populate the updated documents.

When I'd completed a document highlighting where the source information was obtained. I set up a series of drop-in sessions for people to attend so they could start to understand more about the new process and what it meant for their jobs, I took the time to walk them through the new documents that had been developed and the new critical path that supported it. This gave them the opportunity to ask questions and to find out how it all fitted together. The final thing I did was set up one to one meeting with any people who wanted support in completing the documentation for the first time.

By taking the time to fully engage the people who would be using the process and by putting in the level of support that was required, I ensured better process adoption and could make sure that the behaviours needed to ensure successful delivery were also in place.

## It's about them, not you

It's essential that you put yourself in the position of the people who are experiencing the change, and this can only be done by talking to them. It's important that you understand how they are feeling, what concerns them and what their expectations are of you as a leader. This increases your team's sense of psychological safety where people feel free to speak up without fear of repercussion and you as their leader are seen as someone who is willing to do whatever it takes to ensure they feel valued.

Every single person in your business will want to understand three key things:

1. Why is the change happening?
2. What will the future look like?
3. What does it mean for me?

We are all intrinsically selfish and when our personal self-preservation mechanism kicks in, we seek to hold on to what we know and what we feel comfortable with. Therefore, as a leader you need to be able to clearly answer these questions.

### Be prepared to be vulnerable

When leading through change, you need to be prepared to be vulnerable and to admit that you don't have all the answers. Being open, honest, and transparent with your people can go a long way to providing the reassurance that people need.

It's critical that you make time to collect feedback on a regular basis, so you can be sure your people are still on the change journey. Be prepared for some of the feedback you receive to be critical of the way things are being done. Don't take it personally but use it as an opportunity to change the message content, delivery style or frequency. As the old saying goes, 'If there is nothing to say communicate, communicate, communicate.' This will stop people filling any communication gap with what they believe to be true from their own personal narrative. It's very easy for personal perception to become personal reality. Regular check-ins with your people will help avoid this.

### Know your own emotion triggers

It's important that as a leader you understand your own emotional triggers. What frustrates, energises, challenges you on a day-to-day basis? When leading people through change you need to be cognisant of this, so you can be at your best, effectively managing the narrative and communication through your business. It's critical that you show no frustration with your people, as they'll be going through the emotional cycle of change at a different speed to you, ultimately you know what the end result needs to be, and they don't.

If you need to rant and rave, do it behind closed doors with someone you can trust. Let's be honest, who doesn't get frustrated and have the need to blow off steam every now and again?

## Don't set a timetable for leading through the change

What I mean by this is that because individual members of your business will process and navigate their way through the change in different ways and at different speeds you shouldn't identify a date by which you want the change completed. This is different from system, process and governance changes that need to have a defined completion date to allow benefit realisation to start. The key to success is being patient both with yourself and with your people. Be prepared to have multiple conversations, if needed. Different people need differing levels of reassurance and it's your job as their leader to provide it.

Only when people start to produce their work at the level or better than they were prior to the change can you be sure they've moved to the new processes and behaviours.

*'Emotional intelligence grows through perception. Look around at your present situation and observe it through the level of feeling.'*
*Deepak Chopra*

# Leadership Pressure

I dialled my boss's number. It rang for what seemed like an eternity, then finally it connected. The reply was one single word, 'What?' Great, I thought, here we go again!

Sound familiar? You've just encountered a leader who is either:

1. Under massive pressure and stress and sees any interruption as a hassle they can do without; or,
2. Is getting pressure from their boss and passing this pressure on to the people they lead; or,
3. Shouldn't be in a leadership position at all and is there due to length of service or felt pressure to take the job.

The current economic and environmental climate is putting a massive amount of pressure on leaders to be better than they ever have before.

So how as a leader can you ensure you make the time for your people, so both you and they can be effective? I believe that leadership is a privilege, not a chore. Below are three simple steps that you can use to reduce leadership pressure.

## Setting clear accountabilities and expectations

One of the easiest ways of creating time for yourself as a leader is to set clear expectations and accountabilities with all the people that work for you. This should be done from the very first conversation you have with a new hire. As part of any introductory meeting, I have with any new member of my team I always ask them what their expectations are of me as their boss, it then allows me to set my own expectations. Once that conversation has been had both parties are clear about what's needed from the relationship and therefore what they can expect of each other.

I have found the best way to set clear accountabilities is to have an agreed yearly performance plan that clearly sets out what is expected. I would recommend setting one at the beginning of the year and then reviewing it on a quarterly basis. This will ensure that the plan remains relevant and regular conversations are had about performance and the objectives that were agreed at the beginning of the year. Unfortunately, in many cases leaders don't set clear accountabilities with their people and then spend a lot of time having discussions to keep performance on track or even worse many plans are written and then never see the light of day again.

## Regular communication

I have found when I've managed teams that committing to be available whenever your people need you engenders a sense of safety in the team. They know that no matter how busy you are you'll be available to help and support. I have found this a far more effective way of supporting people than having a regular check-in every week where conversations are typically focused on only work and not how the person is feeling, what challenges they're facing and what support they need.

What I've found is that if you start with the person and how they're finding things the work conversation usually drops into the conversation anyway. Ask them about successes they've had and how that made them feel, then focus on the challenges they've experienced and whether there is any support you can offer to help them navigate through it.

## The emotional bank account

Everyone has an emotional bank account and the more you pay in as a leader the more you'll get from your people. It's like paying into a normal bank account the more payments you make the more you'll be able to withdraw when work becomes challenging.

I'll give you a couple of examples from when I managed a small team delivering an aggressive cosmetic merchandising rollout for Boots UK.

One of my Nottingham based team was from Wigan and he'd had a family bereavement. He asked me if he could go and work up north for a few days. My response was no problem, as he had a phone and a laptop. He could do everything as effectively remotely as he could in the office, and he was closer to his family where he felt he needed to be. He came to me at the end of the programme and thanked me for the way I'd line managed him and we still keep in touch now.

Another member of the team was Polish and her mother was coming over for Christmas and her flight arrived in the middle of the afternoon. She asked if she could work from home so she could pick her mum up, I said of course she could, as being able to collect her from the airport was very important. Because I'd enabled her to do what was important to her, she'd often work late to get the work done. I hadn't set this expectation it was simply her working with the freedom that not setting prescriptive hours of work brings.

By allowing them to do what was important to them from an emotional point of view, they went above and beyond expectation when I needed them to. By taking this approach with all members of my team, the programme was delivered on time and under budget. I feel it's critical that you can separate the people who work for you from their jobs they do, allowing them the freedom to work in a way that best suits them. I'm a firm believer that people should be judged on the quality of work that they produce and whether they can hit key deadlines over the hours that they spend working.

I believe that by setting a clear decision-making framework for your people with expectations and accountabilities clearly articulated, you as the leader can give yourself the time and the space to be effective under pressure.

*'It's all about finding the calm in the chaos.'*
***Donna Karan***

## A Wise Monk Once Told Me...

How many times have you as a business leader felt the need to be 100% in control of everything ourselves, the people you lead, the strategies you develop, the performance you need to deliver? I could go on and on; what needs to be thought about, delivered, and reviewed is endless.

What if there was another way, where you don't need to be 100% in control all the time? As a result, you give yourself the permission to move from manager to leader. As awareness in spirituality increases, I genuinely believe there is an opportunity to weave it into a modern leadership style.

I'm sure we've all experienced times in our personal and work lives when we've felt like this, I know I have. In my role as Global Programme Manager for No7 and Skincare in Global Brands at Walgreens Boots Alliance I started to suffer with stress and anxiety due the nature of the role and some of the people I was working for and with. I'd have a sense of dread when things went wrong, or meetings didn't go as I had anticipated. Ultimately, all this pent-up emotion got the better of me to the point where I couldn't handle chairing a meeting we had scheduled with the team in New York. I simply couldn't face entering the room. I left the office, went home, and went for a long bike ride to reflect on what was happening to me. On visiting the doctor, the next day, I was diagnosed with work related stress and was signed off for three weeks.

What this experience taught me was that it's impossible to be in control 100% of the time, that you can forgive yourself when things don't go right and to be brave enough to ask for help when things aren't OK.

To avoid what I went through, below are my five secrets of a Zen leadership style which I believe can remove the daily stress we all face.

### Self-awareness

As a leader, how self-aware are you – I mean truly self-aware? Are you aware of all your emotion triggers, what really pushes your buttons and aggravates you? If you are, do you know how to react in a way that doesn't cause suffering for others, as well as yourself? Do you know what your causes of stress are and how to manage them effectively? It's a simple fact of life that if you keep pushing, sooner or later you'll experience burnout.

So, my challenge to you is. Think about how you can carve an hour out of your busy day just for you, to do something you really love away from work. For me it's yin yoga, which I discovered whilst having to take time off from my other love, cycling, due to hip and lower back pain. I now do it three times a week and the meditative state that it affords me allows me to fully relax before I start a day's work. I can honestly say my stress levels are down, I'm far more reflective and therefore have more control over my thoughts and responses.

If you're in the 'I can't afford the time to' camp, I'd challenge that you can't afford not to. I believe everything is about choices and how you spend your time is a critical one.

## Vulnerability

As I previously touched on, I feel it's important that you can show vulnerability as a leader, that you don't have to have all the answers and your people have a huge part to play in the success of the business. I believe that you must let your people get to know you on more than a work level. What are your core values, your key motivations, and non-negotiables? Society and working relationships have become very transactional, with people's first thought being 'What can you give me?', without any thought to building a long-term robust relationship that will allow for challenging conversations to be had in the future. I believe long standing robust, collaborative relationships can only be built from a place of trust and personal vulnerability is key to this.

I truly believe that to get the best from your people you must show your vulnerability and that in turn will give them the permission to show theirs. You must let your people know that it's OK to get things wrong and that the important thing is to learn from the experience to understand what to do differently next time. The best lessons I've learned in my life have all come from failure. I feel we should welcome failure, not fear it. If you can become comfortable with this, your learning opportunities are endless.

### Compassion

As a leader, it's incredibly important to be able to show compassion to yourself and the people that work for you, I feel it links to your ability to show that you can be vulnerable when seeking to understand what's important.

In my leadership career, I've had examples where you must put people's personal needs before those of the business. If your people know that you see them as more than a cog in a machine and that you value their personal life as much as their work life, you'll have a much more productive colleague as a result.

I would encourage you as a leader to not be a clock-watcher who judges productivity by the number of hours someone works, but judges by the outputs they produce.

### Everything passes

Nothing in life is permanent, not you, me, or the challenges that we face on a day-to-day basis. As a leader, you must learn that success will pass, frustration will pass, even the global pandemic we've lived through has passed. It's been an incredibly tough time for people globally. If you put it into context, the Second World War lasted six years, and one day this, too, passed.

As a leader, you must look beyond your current circumstance to what are the potential opportunities for your business. Ask yourself the question: am I truly doing everything I can to promote and improve my business or am I just hoping for the best? Are you working on your business as much as you're working in it?

I believe that every morning when you get out of bed you choose your mindset: choose how you want to be, choose how you respond to challenges... I could go on and on.

What I'm essentially saying is, don't hang on to physical and emotional attachments for the sake of it. Don't hanker after the past and don't spend too much time worrying about the future. Focus on what you can influence here and now.

**Empathy**

Being truly empathetic with the people who work for you as my friend Neil Lewis, The Empathy Coach, says, 'It is really, really hard.' To do it properly, you must dismiss your own preconceptions, emotions, and reactions to what you believe the other person is feeling and actively listen to the challenges and issues being presented to you.

It's important to understand that it's not about you, it's about them. As leaders, we sometimes leap straight to solution, when in this instance that absolutely isn't what's required.

> *'Every day we are born again.*
> *What we do today matters most.'*
> *The Buddha*

## Boost Your Thinking Time

One thing I have noticed in every single business I've worked in is that there isn't enough time dedicated to thinking. Plenty of time is given to doing; some time is given to reviewing and understanding what to do differently. Unfortunately, thinking never really gets a look-in.

So, what are the benefits of increasing the time that you as leader, your people and your organisation spend thinking. Below I've captured what I believe are the benefits of really sitting down and giving yourself the permission to think.

I feel if we gave as much time to thinking as we do to doing, we wouldn't encounter half the risks, issues, and challenges we often find in business and our day-to-day lives.

### Diarise when you're going to do your thinking

In essence I'm advocating being selfish with your time. We give so much time to others, yet we very rarely give ourselves the chance to sit and think about what we want to achieve on a day-to-day, week-to-week and month-to-month basis. I've taken to blocking time out in my diary so meetings can't be put in my calendar.

This can be an uncomfortable step to take, as colleagues may feel you're being unproductive. I'd contend that it's the exact opposite and that the time you're dedicating to thinking and reflection will make you more productive in the long run.

## Bust the myth

To many people, carving out time in your busy day to think is perceived as doing nothing or being ineffective. I would argue the opposite. Giving yourself the time to envisage what problems you could encounter as you start a piece of work will ultimately save you time in the long run.

Thinking will allow you to consider, 'Who do I need to speak to? What do I need to find out about? How could I engage the people that the work will affect? What will the future look, sound and feel like when the work is done?' Let's be honest, the possibilities are endless.

## Remove all distractions

Turn everything off, email, social media, radio, anything you can think of that will cause a distraction to your thinking time. We've all become slaves to our work email, responding to messages as soon as they come in. Well, guess what: you don't need to. It's only our internal sense of duty that's leading us to do that. Unless an email has a clear timescale for response, I'd suggest answering it when you have time. Social media is the same; we practically have our phones welded to our hands and the number of scrollable apps seems to be increasing by the day. Do yourself a favour: switch it off or put it in another room or do both.

Remove everything tempting and give yourself the unbroken thinking time to plan or deal with what you have on your agenda today. What I've come to understand is that not having outside stimuli bombarding you can really unlock your ability to think deeply and effectively.

## Thinking is doing

It often feels that because thinking isn't a physical activity like writing an email, doing the washing up or going for a run, it carries less importance in our daily lives. I'd like to challenge that notion and put forward a different perspective. Many of the most successful experiences I've had have come from thinking about what a great outcome would be. This could be as simple as thinking about a meeting and anticipating what your stakeholders may need through landing a large-scale transformation programme where I need to think about the communication and engagement strategy, the risks and dependencies, the timescales we're working to and who needs to be involved.

Reflecting on what could happen is often a very good way of identifying challenges you could encounter. This can be anything from people leaving the business in the middle of the initiative you're running through to a supplier you're using going out of business. By doing this you're designing a blueprint for increased success, as you have a plan for most of the issues you could encounter. As the saying goes, 'Forewarned is forearmed.'

## It can turbo charge your business

Consider what it is you want from your life, your relationships, your job, your business. Do we really give ourselves the time to consider this or do we just drift from day to day without really having a clue where we're going?

I know when I started The Change Partner, I knew I needed to change my current situation. The thing is, I didn't go straight into doing it. I thought about what I wanted the business to provide for others. This thinking and conversations with people I really trust got me to the position you see today. It's one I'm proud of and the beginning was starting with the end in mind, which is – you've guessed it – thinking.

## Embrace the great outdoors

How often do we find our minds full of noise, conflicting priorities, conversations we need to have, jobs we need to do? One of the most effective ways that I've found of clearing my head is going for a walk. Even if it's for just 10 minutes, the change in surroundings and stimuli can very often provide the time and space for you to think without distraction. So, go ahead, embrace Mother Nature, or take a trip to the shops.

*'Take time to think; it is the source of power.'*
*Author unknown*

## Sure-Fire Ways to Engage Your People

In the fast-paced world that we all live and work in, engaging your people as a leader has never been more critical to the success of your business.

Engaged people will go beyond what is expected and will become the cornerstone of your business and its success. Your people are your most prized asset and taking the time to engage them will reap huge dividends.

### Personal reason why

Everybody has a reason for being at work, and as a leader you should seek to understand why. There will be various reasons. It may be that they are keen to build a career and progress to a leadership position; it could be that they have a family, and they are their primary focus, and their job is a way of supporting their family. Whatever their reason, you need to find a way of engaging them in where they fit in the company's strategy and priorities and how the role, they perform can help you create a successful business.

### Towards motivation

When looking to engage people in the direction of the business it should be done with motivation that takes you towards something, rather than away from. What I mean by this is where is the business heading in terms of success factors, e.g. 'We are looking to drive a 10% uplift in sales by

30th April 2023, as measured by sales being 10% higher than last year,' instead of 'We're losing sales and we need to improve them to ensure we remain viable.'

Can you see the difference? The first is a clear objective that people can understand and measure; the second lacks clarity and has no clear way of helping your people understand where they fit in and how they can contribute. By giving your people clear collective and individual objectives, you'll increase their engagement and therefore their productivity. As I've touched on previously, this is also an ideal opportunity to define accountabilities and set clear expectations.

### Individual values

As we covered in previous chapters seeking to understand what your people value on an individual level, what's important to them is the way that you and the business conducts itself towards them. It could be honesty, integrity, transparency, consistent communication. Whatever it is, it's important that you know what these are so you can ensure that your company embodies what your people feel it should. Ultimately, if people feel you aren't interested or don't care about their values, it's likely they'll be unproductive and may finally leave your business to find one that better matches their values and individual motivations.

## Development opportunities

What personal development opportunities can you provide for your people either in the role they currently do or with a mind to improving their long-term prospects? People are generally motivated by more than just money and giving them the chance to challenge themselves on a personal and a working level should increase their engagement with what you're looking to achieve as the leader. It is important, however, to provide a supportive framework, with regular check-ins where support is offered to ensure the development experience is one the person enjoys. It's your accountability as the leader to ensure this happens. Creating an environment where mistakes are acceptable, and growth can happen is vitally important. All my best learning experiences have come from mistakes I've made. The key is to reflect on what needs to be done differently, making the necessary changes to be successful in the future. These openings for self-improvement will also provide your people with the chance to be involved, strengthening their commitment to what you want to do.

## Sunday night feeling

We've all had it, the Sunday night feeling when Monday morning looms and the thought of work enters our heads. How can you remove this feeling of dread that we all experience from time to time? Could you have your team meetings on a Monday morning to get a sense of people's personal energies? How can you help set them up for success for the rest of the week? What will kickstart the week for each of your people? Ask your people what they feel will get their week off to the perfect start.

> ***'When people are financially invested, they want a return. When people are emotionally invested, they want to contribute.'***
> ***Simon Sinek***

## Guarantees To Make Your Meetings Better

Now let's be completely honest, we've all sat in meetings that have been a complete waste of time, with no sense of direction, no clear idea of what's being discussed, people on phones not paying attention... I could go on and on.

My most successful meetings have always been the ones that I've thought about and prepared for, they have been shorter, more productive and lead to a clear way forward for the work that needs to be done.

Many of these points may be obvious, however I've been in enough meeting to assure you that they don't happen. Here are my guaranteed ways to make your meetings a hell of a lot better!

### Mobile phone etiquette

If there is one thing that irritates me more than anything else in meetings, its people believing it's OK to be on their mobile phone while in a meeting. I'm not sure how these individuals are paying 100% attention to what's going on; let's be honest, they can't. A sure-fire way to overcome this is to insist that all phones are either off or on silent and placed in the middle of the table. This will remove the temptation to be texting, writing an email or reviewing social media feeds. I've even been in a company briefing where a senior manager was watching YouTube!

## Have an agenda

Sounds obvious, doesn't it, having a document that describes what's going to be talked about, what the objectives of the meeting are and what decisions need to be made? I've lost count of the meetings that I've been in where people have little to no clue what's being talked about and an hour later when the meeting is over people still have no clue what was agreed.

Personally, I feel an agenda is an absolute necessity for all meetings and it should be circulated prior to the meeting so people know what will be discussed, the timings and what they will be expected to contribute. Having the decisions that are needed from the meeting captured will also ensure that the meeting delivers the right outcomes. If you have nothing else for your meeting, make sure you have an agenda!

## Have someone keep time

Another problem that is encountered in meetings is that they run over and either it never gets finished, or people must leave, or people are asked if they can continue, which in a lot of instances they can't. This is easily fixed by having someone track time against what's been captured on the agenda. It's also important not to be afraid to take a conversation offline and outside the meeting if it's consuming time that has been put aside to discuss another agenda item.

## Check attendance and have meeting delegates

How many times do you get everyone to attend your meetings? Somewhere between not ever and never. I have always insisted that a delegate is sent to a meeting, so a certain function is represented, and actions can be captured and allocated to that department. Better still, if you can get a delegate with the same decision rights as the original person you've struck gold, as there will be no need for a further conversation outside the meeting. It makes the whole meeting decision-making process much more effective and meaningful. I would also recommend checking meeting attendance at least two days prior to the meeting date, so you can have a conversation to get any delegates in place. If a delegate can't be provided, people may need to understand that they won't be able to voice their opinion in the decision-making process.

## Capturing Actions Accurately

I'm sure we've all done it; I know I have. You've finished a meeting and you look at the notes you've captured, and you can't tell the difference between actions, decisions or simply things you have written to reflect on after the meeting has finished. The way I ensure I know which the actions are is by putting an A with a circle round it in red pen next to what you've written. I also ensure I know who the action has been assigned to and the date that the action needs to be completed by. I've been doing this for the best part of 20 years, and I've found it an easy and effective way of ensuring you're clear on what needs to be done because of the conversation that's been had. I would also recommend doing a review of the actions you've captured at the end of the meeting to ensure everyone is clear about what's expected of them. I would also advocate the use of a RAID (risks, actions, issues, and decisions) log used to capture these. These actions should then be circulated at the no later than two days after the meeting, so people have time to review the actions assigned to them and that they have done them or have an update.

> *'Time is really the only capital that any human being has and the thing he can't afford to lose.'*
> *Thomas Edison*

### Check out your meeting room

We've all experienced this: you book a room and it's too small. The result is people looking for chairs in other meeting rooms, standing up or sitting on the floor. Your meeting looks more like a gig, with people focusing more on their comfort than the topic that's being discussed. I would encourage you to check out the room and if it's too small get people to dial into the meeting via phone or video.

Also, always check out the equipment in the room. How many times have you seen someone go to use a flipchart and one of two things happens: no paper or the pen has dried up with only a visit to an optician enabling you to see the words? If you know you need paper and pens, take them to the meeting with you.

## Check phone and video conference technology works

We've all seen it or suffered it: you go into a meeting room to use phone or video conference facilities and they don't work. Cue frantic rooting under the table to find which cable isn't plugged in. Unfortunately, people have had to see my backside sticking in the air on more than one occasion while I've frantically tried to sort it out. Or there's a panicked call to IT because the video conference isn't working, and you have people from the other side of the globe trying to dial in.

The solution is dead simple. First thing in the morning, I would take a walk and check all rooms I had booked, and all the tech was working. It could take 10 minutes first thing in the morning, but it reduced my stress levels massively.

## Do you need a meeting at all?

We've all become conditioned to believing that a meeting is the only way to get a decision made. With the introduction of live messaging tools such as Slack or Teams, it's much easier to reach a consensus on a simple question without having to get people in a room to come to the same conclusion. It's also easier and simpler to go and ask a person a question if you're in an office environment. So, ask yourself: do I really need the meeting or is it just a force of habit that's making me put the time in people's diaries to get the answer I need?

## Meeting Lengths

We live in a world where diaries can be filled from the first to the last minute of the day, every day of the week. Did you know that you can change the default length of the meetings via the settings in your calendar?

Making your meetings 50 or 55 minutes long will achieve three things:

1. It'll give people breathing space between meetings to grab a drink or go to the toilet.
2. It'll reduce the number of times people are late for your meetings.
3. It'll reduce stress levels as people will see breaks between meetings instead of the solid block, we all often experience.

## Managing non-attendance

Every single person who has organised a meeting has experienced this: somebody who simply didn't turn up, no apology, no warning, just didn't turn up. Now, the temptation with these individuals is to give them a hard time about not turning up, saying you needed their input, etc. I've found this can be ineffective and can cause you stress, as you need to have an uncomfortable conversation.

I've found a far more effective way is to speak with the person concerned to make sure they are OK. There could have been a genuine reason for them missing the meeting. This allows you to do two things: if the reason is legit, you can empathise with the person concerned and show that you're interested in their wellbeing; or if there isn't a genuine reason, it's much easier to highlight the importance of attendance and it's a much more comfortable way of holding someone to account.

## Managing long meetings

We've all done it: we've seen a long meeting go in the diary and thought, 'OMG, it's going to be torture having to be in a meeting that long.' We only have a limited attention span and by the end of a two to three-hour meeting most people are physically and mentally exhausted. Two ways of making this easier on the participants are: to communicate that there will be breaks in the meeting to allow them to get a drink and go to the toilet; or to consider whether two shorter meetings would be more effective, enabling people's attention spans to be better managed.

*'The amount of meetings I've been in – people would be shocked. But that's how you gain experience, how you can gain knowledge, being in meetings and participating. You learn and grow.'*
**Tiger Woods**

# Cornerstones

## Difference Between Change, Programme and Project Management

Whilst change, programme and project management may seem very similar, some may feel even the same, they are in fact very different. Let me explain.

### Change management

As I've previously covered, change management is driven by a reason. This could range from poor business performance through to a change in industry regulation that requires a change to be made to remain compliant. When making a personal or business change there are many considerations to be made, ranging from how you plan to engage and communicate with the people affected, to planning and execution, and finally integration into business as usual.

As I have highlighted elsewhere in this book, when making any change it needs to be thoroughly thought through, with a clear plan detailed to increase your chances of success. It's very easy for change to fail, and to effectively deliver a change initiative and make it stick you must have a plan to tackle the following:

1. Have you clearly defined the reason why you're making the change and what your goals are? Short, medium, and long term.
2. Do you have a plan for all phases, from initiation, through to mobilisation, execution and finally realisation?
3. Have you clearly defined your priorities, and what task you are going to do first? Aim to start this within 24 hours of finishing your list.
4. Who or what can also help you make your change initiative a true success? Think outside the box.

As we have seen earlier, change also has a highly emotive element attached to it as the people affected by what's happening will either readily accept, deny, or flatly refuse to acknowledge what is being proposed. I would encourage you to put your people at the heart of any organisational change as they will either be your biggest advocate or your biggest critic.

### Programme Management

The Association of Project Management (APM) defines programme management as the coordinated management of projects and business-as-usual activities to achieve beneficial change. A programme is a unique and transient strategic endeavour undertaken to achieve a beneficial change and incorporating a group of related projects and business-as-usual activities.

In my own experience programmes are typically run-in large organisations where there are multiple functions affected by the change that is being instigated. I've found that they are very resource hungry and if the correct level of resource isn't committed to and if the people doing the work are doing so on top of their day job the programme will very quickly go off track. I've experienced this in one of the companies I worked with and within three months the projects within the programme had been delayed. One had gone back 3 months due to issues that needed fixing in base business, and one had gone back nine months due to the delays experienced with getting the right people into meetings to understand the technology requirements to build a new system to support the business. In the second example here, the dependency of the milestones on each other is what was impacted: once the first milestone was pushed back, it had a knock-on effect to the next five resulting in the nine-month delay.

I would recommend before any programme is started that the number of people needed to complete the work is fully understood. This may mean that you need to back-fill roles so people can be released to focus on the programme or bring in external people to support. I would also recommend that the budget is agreed and committed to before any resource requirements are decided upon. When backfilling existing people in the business I would suggest starting with the most senior person needed and work back from there.

As an example, if you need to release 50% of a Trading Directors time to commit to a programme, reflect on whether the Head of Trading can pick up that 50%, if they can you would then need to release 50% of the Head of Trading's role and so on and so forth until you get to a role that could be more easily filled. As an example, this could be a temporary Trading Assistant who could cost in the region of £30k for 12 months.

What many businesses fail to recognise is the loss of benefits by not delivering initiatives on time and how the cost of these losses far outweighs the cost of getting the right number of people in to complete the work. Literally millions of pounds in lost benefit and productivity can be experienced simply because companies don't understand the importance of a robust resource framework.

Programmes are complex with many risks, dependencies, issues, and actions some of which span across more than one programme. I'll cover later in the book the need to have a robust governance framework in place and the benefits it will bring. All I would say at this point is that if your business is running a programme of any size ensure the people accountable for leading each workstream speak to each other on a regular basis I would advocate monthly as a minimum. This will ensure that visibility of dependencies and risks remains in alignment and that any issues that arise can be quickly and effectively dealt with.

## Project management

Project management is the defined delivery of an initiative it could range from introducing a new piece of technology into your business through to arranging a wedding. A project has a defined start and end point and has a set of tasks that need to be completed to make it a success. It's the process of leading a piece of work through a team of people to achieve an agreed objective within an agreed timeframe to an agreed standard. Where it differs from change and programme management is that typically it requires no business-wide engagement, and the impact is smaller than that of a business-wide change programme.

I believe project and programme management is a mechanism to deliver change, and any large-scale change initiatives should be broken down into distinct projects that have their own set of objectives, deliverables, timescales, risks, etc.

When delivering a project, there should be a standard suite of documents that are used to ensure its success. These should include action, risk, and issue logs, a top-line milestone plan and a detailed project plan outlining who's accountable for what and by when. I've always found it important to create a stakeholder map, as previously described in the book. It ensures that everyone you come into contact with is aligned to the objectives and is clear on the direction the work is heading in.

Projects help you deliver an individual objective, whilst change supports a longer-term vision and strategy. Ultimately, how effectively you plan and deliver change will be a greater predictor of your future individual and business success.

*'Be not afraid of going slowly,*
*be afraid only of standing still.'*
*Chinese proverb*

# The Secret to Successful Project Management

Effective project management is one of the key criteria to having a successful business. If you can deliver them effectively and on time, to standard and to budget, the opportunities to bring success to your business increase dramatically. They are part of your everyday life, from preparing a new dish for a group of friends, through to having an extension built on your house. Anything that has a defined start and finish can be classed as a project.

The dictionary defines a project as, 'something that is contemplated, devised, or planned'. So pretty much everything in our lives can be defined as a project if you think hard enough about it. Even your marriage or relationship is an ongoing project that has objectives, a plan, a need for engagement and communication and periodic reviews. I know mine is.

In this section, I'll highlight what I believe needs to be in place to guarantee successful projects time after time.

## How project management works

I believe projects work best within a defined and agreed framework such as Waterfall or Agile or a combination of the two. Qualifications such as Prince2 or Association of Project Management (APM) can help with this. The most important thing is that all stakeholders know where they fit in and how they contribute. Without this, I feel projects lack direction and ultimately fail to deliver the expected benefits, so in defining your governance framework and what you should put in place, I would recommend that as a minimum you have weekly project meetings and a monthly steering group defined before the project starts.

I would also recommend that the agreed methodology is in place before you start the engagement of key functions and people. Not having this in place from the beginning will result in delays to the work starting and a lack of clarity on what needs to happen first.

## Where is project management used?

In my opinion, project management can be used in all areas of a business from manufacturing to supply chain through to commercial and marketing. During my time at DFS, it was one of the cornerstones that was used to successfully deliver the strategy the leaders of the business had defined. As highlighted above, I believe project management is a framework that can be applied to all businesses and any organisational function.

## The project sponsor

The sponsor is key to the success of any project. This is the person who has asked for the work to be done and they should be ultimately accountable for its success or failure. In short, the buck stops with them!

The sponsor typically also sets the key goals and objectives for the project as well as agreeing the budget, allocating the resource, and agreeing the timescales that the project needs to be delivered against.

The sponsor will also be one of the key decision-makers during the life of the project and will usually chair the monthly steering group meeting. Their key accountability in these meetings is to ensure that the project remains on track by removing blockers, resolving resource issues, and making decisions on change requests that may impact on the budget and agreed completion date.

### Subject matter experts

As the project manager, you are the conductor of the orchestra, with the job of ensuring that the work gets delivered on time, to the required standard and within the agreed budget. To deliver the day-to-day activity of the project, subject matter experts need to be provided by the business, ideally on a full-time basis. This will ensure that the work gets the focus it needs. Ideally, you should have a subject matter expert from every part of the business that the project touches and they should be the person who gets information from their functional area to feed into the project. They should also be accountable for ensuring any project actions are completed by themselves or by someone who works in their department. Essentially, they are your person facing back into their functional area who will be able to keep their colleagues informed of how the work is progressing, they should also be accountable for gathering any feedback and getting any questions answered to enable the work to progress. They will be critical to the success of your project.

### Project governance

It's essential that a robust governance framework is in place to increase your chances of success, this should cover both meetings and documents. Your meeting and document structure should be sufficient to satisfy the key stakeholders in your business, but not be onerous to the point of paralysis where it feels like the only thing that's being achieved is the production of documents and reports for senior leaders. Striking this balance is crucial, as the information needs to provide the right level to inspire confidence in the project whilst remaining agile enough to achieve the agreed goals and dates. Ideally the information that is generated by the project should be suitable for all audiences from Senior Leaders to the Project Team. If you can agree what the expectations are before the work starts it makes this much easier to accomplish when the project is in flight.

### Meetings

In my experience, a clearly defined meeting structure is essential to the success of all projects. This needs to include the following:

## Risk workshop

It's best practice to hold a risk workshop at the beginning of every project. It enables all the subject matter experts who will make up the project team to feed in any risks that they feel will be detrimental to the success of the project. I have found that the most effective way to run a risk workshop is as follows:

1. Ask all those attending to capture their risks on Post-it Notes prior to the meeting.

2. During the meeting, the impact of the risk on the project needs to be captured using a high, medium or low ranking. I would suggest this is done on a flipchart. The same then needs to be done for how likely the chances of risk occurring are. Again, this should be done using a high, medium or low ranking. I would suggest this is also done on a flipchart.

3. The risks need to be ranked against the company's internal risks matrix if there is one. If not, review the risks as a group and agree which are the most likely to happen and how much damage could they do to the delivery of the project. For example, if a risk is highly likely to happen and it's an absolute showstopper, then it needs to be ranked high.

4. Once all the risks have been ranked, the next step is to agree the mitigating action that needs to be taken, as

well as the owner of the risk and when it will be reviewed.

5. Risks should then be typed up into your risk log and reviewed on a weekly basis in the project meeting.

## Steering group

The steering group is where the decision-makers of the project meet to understand and assess the health of the project. It should solely be used as a decision-making forum and should provide the clarity the project needs to move forward, should there be any issues. The type of issues this forum should look to resolve are resource issues, unresolved conflicts, blockers to progress such as additional budget requirements, risks that have significantly increased and pose a threat to project delivery and any change requests that will affect the time, cost, or quality of the project.

The key milestones should also be reviewed using the Plan on a Page (covered below) to ensure the project is on track to deliver against the key benefits outlined in the scope document. It's also important to understand if any key milestones have slipped and what the overall impact on the project is, as there could be key dependencies between your milestones.

## Weekly project meetings

Weekly project meetings are critical to the success of any project; they give the project team the opportunity to meet to discuss the progress of the work. They are the detailed sessions that deal with the weekly actions resulting from the work in progress and the risks that have been identified in the risk workshop. The detailed time plan also needs to be reviewed in the meeting. The weekly project meeting also provides the main opportunity for the project manager to hold the project team accountable to the actions they've committed to. Holding the tension on the project deliverables is the project manager's accountability and the weekly meeting is the opportune time to do it. I've always found that being open, honest, and direct in these meetings has produced the best results. It's the project manager's accountability to make sure the project delivers on time, and this may require difficult conversations to be had if things aren't going to plan.

## Dependency identification

If the project you're running is part of a wider programme, it's likely that you'll have dependencies on activity in other projects. It's critical that these are identified at the outset so they can be effectively managed and any potential impacts on key milestone timings can be understood.

There are typically five types of dependencies and I've detailed them below:

## Logical

Also known as causal dependencies, these dependencies are an inherent part of the project and cannot be avoided. Tasks characterised as logical dependency usually use the output of the preceding tasks as input so you can't run them in parallel.

Consider baking a cake as your project; you can't start the process unless you have all the ingredients you need.

## Resources

This dependency originates from a project constraint, as it deals with the availability of shared resources. If two tasks require the same resource for completion, then they'll each be dependent on the completion of the other.

## Preferential

These dependencies generally depend on the team members, other stakeholders and industrial practices. Preferential dependencies arise when tasks are scheduled to follow developed standard practices.

In most cases, the project can be completed even if you ignore the preferential dependencies in your tasks, but there will be some quality issues.

### External

No matter how much you plan, there are things bound to be out of your control. Some tasks are dependent on outside factors, and project managers can't do anything to influence their project progress to deal with these dependencies. It's recommended to have a backup plan.

Delays from the suppliers or other unforeseen circumstances may take place, which can affect your progress. A good project manager always makes some contingency plans so everything keeps running smoothly even in the face of adversity.

### Cross-functional

This is a common occurrence in large organisations. Sometimes multiple teams work on a single, complex project and they rely on each other to complete the project on time. Effective project time management can be implemented to avoid long hours. It's important that you meet on a regular basis with the other project managers to ensure you understand if the dependencies you are relying on will still be delivered to the original timescales. Failure to do this will result in unexpected impacts on your project.

## Project documentation

I have run many successful projects both in the UK and globally and I believe without the following documents delivering successfully becomes exceedingly difficult.

### Scope document

Every project needs to have a scope document, as it details what the project is designed to deliver. It could be as basic as detailing the objectives, what's in and out of scope, what the key milestones are, who the key stakeholders are, the key risks, and assumptions, through to a MoSCoW (Must have, Should have, Could have, Won't have this time) scoping document as used in agile project methodology. It's a very effective way of getting clarity on what the key project deliverables are and where your initial priorities should be.

The scope document should be used as the central reference document for the project, ensuring that the objectives initially agreed are being delivered and that scope creep doesn't happen. Scope creep is when a project changes without formal agreement, it often comes from a senior leader in the business who sees the project as a way of delivering a personal objective or delivering additional benefit without considering the impact to the original project scope.

## Business case

Essentially, any project that doesn't have a clearly defined business case highlighting the benefits of the work shouldn't get off the start line. The business case should be used to inform the business whether the work is worth doing at all. It can be used to measure all kinds of metrics from purely financial to the design, development and implementation of a new system or software. Ideally, it should be completed by the person accountable for the financial wellbeing of the company and it should be signed off by the project sponsor or business owner before work commences. Failure to have a robust business case makes it impossible to review the success of the project. This can often lead to recrimination and finger-pointing if the expected benefits aren't realised.

I've inherited numerous projects that didn't have a robust business case detailing the cost as well as the benefit and when I started to scrutinise the validity of doing the work a convincing answer often couldn't be given. A decision then needed to be made on whether the project would be paused until a business case was completed. A project without a clear business case therefore runs a greater risk of failure and of being stopping altogether as the benefits can't be proved or the costs can't be accurately assessed.

## RAID log (Risks, Actions, Issues and Decisions)

I believe the RAID log, along with the project plan, is the most critical document used to run a project. It should be used to capture all the risks and mitigating actions that have been captured in the risk workshop. Every action coming out of the weekly project meeting should also be captured, with an owner and completion date. If these are missing, holding people to account becomes very difficult to do. Any open issues also need to be captured and worked through to completion. If you have done a comprehensive risk review, you should encounter very few of these. Finally, the decisions need to be captured accurately as they form a record of what has been agreed and by who. I worked on numerous projects and programmes where this hasn't happened and as a result the work can be delayed as the same conversation needs to be had sometimes with a different outcome. This can ultimately cause costly delays to the work, resulting in an increase in cost, a reduction in quality as the work is rushed to achieve an agreed deadline or an increase in the time needed to deliver the work.

## POAP (Plan on a Page)

The milestone POAP is a document that is used to keep the senior leaders of the business informed about how work is tracking against the key activity. It should highlight what has been completed, what's on track to be delivered to the agreed timescales, and what is off track and how long the work will be delayed. It should be used in the steering group and any board meetings to facilitate a conversation on what needs to happen to support the progress of the initiative. The POAP should also highlight any dependencies on other work and projects. This should be done in a table sitting underneath the plan.

### Project plan

Any project that doesn't have a plan is doomed to failure; it's a fundamental requirement. If no plan is in place, you run the risk of your project missing key deadlines, which will ultimately impact the benefits case. In my experience, the most robust project plans are co-created with the cross-functional project team, as this will give them a real sense of ownership and a shared sense of accountability. Also, a joint plan is not just seen as the project manager's accountability.

The plan should detail every piece of activity needed to deliver the project, the what, the when and the who. I know I keep stressing this, but without these in place it's impossible to hold people accountable for their work. If you're the project manager, don't be afraid of pushing for all the details and take pride in holding the tension in the plan, there's also nothing wrong with ruffling a few feathers occasionally.

## Meeting agenda

As I highlighted earlier, we've all sat in meetings that seem to go on forever as they have no objective and no direction. This can easily be avoided if you get in the habit of producing an agenda for every meeting that you hold. It should clearly state who's attending, the discussion points of the meeting, how long each agenda item will run for and who will lead the conversation. When in the meeting it's also best practice to have a timekeeper to ensure that agenda items don't run over. If this does happen, don't be afraid to intervene and suggest that another conversation is warranted to keep the meeting moving.

## Change request

Once the scope and budget for the project have been agreed, any requests to make change should be managed through a formal change control process. This will ensure that scope creep can be avoided, and as a result the integrity of the business case can be maintained.

The change control process should be used to capture any proposed changes that could affect the time, cost or quality of the agreed scope. Once the request has been received, all three of these metrics should be thoroughly assessed before the change request is accepted or refused. I have found that senior leaders can be notorious for asking for change to projects without understanding the impact; using a formal process gives everyone the chance to pause for breath, ensuring the right decision is reached.

## Status Report

The final report, which is needed as the status report, essentially, it's a health check on what's happening in the project you're running. It should provide a summary of the work and its purpose is to facilitate discussions in the steering group.

It needs to capture at a high level what progress has been made over the month, what issues are being encountered and what support is needed to resolve them, which risks have increased and either need closer scrutiny or a fresh set of mitigating actions. Solutions should also be proposed for the issues and risks that have been pulled out as important. This will allow the sponsor and other key people to form an opinion on whether what you're suggesting is feasible and if not, it'll open the opportunity to have a clear conversation on what needs to happen.

I have used status reports in various formats from a basic template detailing the subject matter highlighted above through a more complex structure that use red, amber, green (RAG) status to give prominence to the areas that require increased focus to keep them on track.

*'First, have a definite, clear, practical ideal – a goal, an objective. Second, have the necessary means to achieve your ends – wisdom, money, materials and methods. Third, adjust all your means to that end.'*
*Aristotle*

## Case Study

### Project Sweetshop – Boots UK

Whilst working for a company called Momentum Instore, I led a small team on behalf of Boots UK delivering a merchandising programme to replace every piece of self-selection cosmetics furniture in their 2,500 shops. The total number of bays we needed to change were 26.500 and the total number of individual parts was over a million. We had two manufacturers to work with one in China and the other in Poland, three merchandising installation companies and thirteen cosmetics brands including L'Oreal and Revlon and we had an implementation window of just 6 months. A few people doubted it was possible, as something of this size and scale had never been achieved in such a short time frame.

The key to its success was the intense planning phase that was at the beginning of the programme, this enabled key stakeholders to be fully engaged, thorough risk workshops to be held to identify things that could go wrong during the life of the programme and a clear implementation schedule to be drafted that all the merchandising partners had given feedback on and had therefore fully bought into.

The programme was set up with a robust governance structure that included weekly working groups with the manufacturers, merchandising companies, and all the cosmetics brands. This ensured we kept track of all the risks, issues and actions associated with each stakeholder and that they could be quickly and effectively addressed. There was also a monthly meeting held between Boots and the partners delivering the programme to ensure that key issues could be raised and resolved, this ensured that the focus remained on what was important to deliver the work.

We did encounter issues during the programme, the main one was when the manufacturer in China had problems with what they were producing. Fortunately, we had identified this as one of the biggest risks to the programme so when it did happen, we had a plan, which was to move some of production to Poland while they corrected the issues. This ensured that the September deadline that had been agreed could still be achieved.

One of the key things I learnt from this programme was that it's important to go slowly in the beginning to go faster at the end. Taking the time to plan things effectively saves so much time when the project or programme is running as in many cases you have the solution documented, meaning all you need to do is apply it to the situation.

Project Sweetshop was easily the most challenging and rewarding programme I have ever worked on and by applying many of the principles I've described we delivered the programme on time, to the required standard and under budget. It was also nominated and won the Gold Award for Project Management at the 2019 POPAI awards and if you go into any Boots store you can see what was achieved for yourself.

> *"Change is hardest at the beginning, messiest in the middle and best at the end"*
> *Robin.S.Sharma*

## Conclusion

The principles and ideas you've just read are designed to help you envision, define, mobilse and implement the business or personal change you want to make. They will enable you to effectively engage and energise yourself and your people to ensure it's completed in a way that ensures you're ambitions are set in place for the long term and continue to support sustainable growth.

As you embark on your change journey you're likely to find different elements useful, so the book is designed to work as an end to end guide to help you obtain your goals or to be picked up and put down whilst taking the salient points you need in order to move forward. As you will have read I believe that people need to be at the heart of any change or transformation which is why I've concentrated heavily on the personal aspects of change. From you the leader through to every person in your business everyone has a need to understand what's happening and why. This mustn't be underestimated.

You will find accomplishing your objectives difficult at times and this will take personal resilience to deal with, I would encourage you to accept failure as part of the learning process and to give yourself permission to not get things right 100% of the time. Giving yourself personal time will keep you focused, motivated and will provide the breathing space you'll need to think and reflect on what has been done and what is still to come.

Going slowly in the beginning and thoroughly thinking through what you want to do and how you can achieve it will increase your probability of success. Thinking through the risks and planning what could go wrong are invaluable exercises and will provide you with a blueprint to deal with the bumps in the road you'll encounter. Be more tortoise and less hare and you won't go far wrong.

So what's my final message? Change is inevitable and shouldn't be feared. It's what drives innovation, adaptation and personal growth. Yes it can be complicated, messy and unpredictable however the difference at the end can be ground breaking, life changing or spiritually uplifting. I would encourage you to embrace change to realise your personal and business aspirations. So, enjoy exploring change you won't regret it.

**'The price of doing the same old thing is far higher than the price of change'**
**Bill Clinton**

# Testimonials

## Jonathan Grainger – Head of Business Change, DFS

Simon joined DFS to work with me as part of a small team to deliver a step-change in how we plan for and manage delivery of change across our portfolio of transformation programmes.

From day one he has built great relationships with stakeholders at all levels and worked across multiple programmes to ensure plans are in place, people are clear on the part they play in delivery, and that we track progress in a way that works for the business.

He has also been hugely supportive to me in helping to shape and implement a programme management framework and governance structure that has worked very effectively in a business that was relatively immature in managing major change.

He would be an asset to any business on a similar change journey to ours and I'd like to thank him for everything he has done.

## Philippa McNamara – Managing Director, Kin Ltd

It's been my absolute pleasure and privilege to work with Simon again, and proof positive as to why I approached him to support our journey of transformation at Wilko.

As well as being a highly skilled and experienced leader in portfolio programme management, Simon brings out the best in everyone around him. With a natural coaching style and generous interest in advancing both business goals and individual progress, Simon has added tremendous value to our team.

From day one until the end of his contract, Simon has demonstrated the commitment of a permanent employee (and then some). And I can't remember the last time I've been stopped by so many colleagues expressing how much they have valued the contribution of a contractor.

Thank you all you've done to set us up for success Simon!

## Rachel Panther – Managing Director, PrimarySite

Simon joined PrimarySite at the beginning of July to support the development of the project governance and management area of the business. From day one Simon worked to understand what we needed to improve these functions and he quickly developed a plan that would enable both the processes and the people to develop in their roles.

As early as the first week he had established a project scope document that enabled us to prioritise projects that were right for customer and that would deliver the right commercial return. Simon also helped set up a business wide Steering Group and reporting structure to ensure the right projects were being discussed and that risks, issues and dependencies could be effectively managed. Before Simon came into the business we had started using a project payback model to assess the projects we were delivered, he worked with us to improve this further, we now feel we have model that will enable us to make the right decisions going forward.

Simon has also spent time coaching and mentoring our project managers and we have seen a step change in how they organise, prepare and chair meetings, bringing clarity to the process. He has also agreed to continue providing this to us as and when it's required.

I would highly recommend Simon for any business looking to make change, his ability to quickly understand what's required, coupled with his talent for building a bespoke solution make him a leader in the business change field.

## Richard Powell – Head of Programme Management, Holland and Barrett

Simon worked for Holland and Barrett for over 12 months, he is a first-class programme manager. Simon possesses an excellent blend of functional and commercial business knowledge whilst maintaining oversight and control over complex programme delivery plans. One of Simon's key strengths are his stakeholder management skills. He has the ability to influence at all levels of the organisation up to C-suite and exudes confidence when dealing with senior leadership within the business. Simon is very open to sharing his skills and knowledge with more junior project and programme managers and is always willing to support and advise.

I would highly recommend Simon to any organisation seeking a top-class programme manager.

## Andy Tweedale – Director of Store Customer Service, DFS

I worked with Simon at DFS and in our time working together we made improvements to the company's customer service provision. Simon gets 'it'. Our coffee break discussions were where ideas flowed and plans were made and most importantly the action, the hard work, doing the things we said we would, led to great improvements. As with any change it's critical to stick to the project and see it through – this is where Simon excelled, making certain that yesterday's brilliant ideas became tomorrow's benefit, to the customer and to the business. Simon is passionate and unyielding when it comes to doing the right thing and sticking to the program and as a seriously brilliant communicator can engage with people at all levels to ensure delivery through people.

*'If you want change, you have to make it. If we want progress we have to drive it'*
*Susan Rice*

## Suggestions for Additional Reading

I've read many books on change and other subjects whilst on my personal journey. These are some of my favourites, in no particular order:

1. **The 7 Habits of Highly Effective People** by Stephen R Covey. This was the first book I read many years ago when I first became interested in my personal development. The principles in the book and how it's structured give you a step-by-step guide to understand where your opportunities for self-improvement lie.

2. **They Ask You Answer** by Marcus Sheridan. I got the idea of writing blogs as a form of inbound marketing after reading this book; the blogs also form the basis of much of my book. If you truly want to understand how to deliver content marketing effectively, this is the book to get hold of.

3. **Switch** by Chip and Dan Heath. This is a great book if you want to understand how your analytical brain and emotional heart both play a part in delivering successful change. It's written in a way that's easy to access and highlights plenty of case studies on how to deliver effective change.

4. **Talk Lean** by Alan H Palmer. At times we all tend not to say what we mean through fear of offending someone.

This book is a practical guide on how to get the most from the conversations you have, helping you to understand how to get straight to the point without appearing rude.

5. **Start with Why** by Simon Sinek. Everything must start with a reason why. This global bestseller highlights how great leaders are the key to success and how the Golden Circle of Why, How and What link to how your brain works.

6. **Go MAD – The Art of Making a Difference** by Andy Gilbert. One of the first books I read on how to enable successful change, this book provides a tried and tested methodology to delivering successful change in organisations of all sizes.

7. **How to Win Friends and Influence People** by Dale Carnegie. An old book first published in 1936, all of it still holds true today. If you want to understand how to be effective in your personal relationships and how this can shape business success, get yourself a copy.

8. **High Performance – Lessons from the Best on Becoming Your Best** by Jake Humphrey and Professor Damian Hughes. This is a brilliant book based on a highly successful podcast. The book takes you through some of the most successful people in the world and highlights that everyone experiences failure. It's what we learn from it that matters.

9. **The Heart of the Buddha's Teaching** - Thich Nhat Hanh, I read this book during the first Covid19 lockdown in the UK and it really resonated with me. It's principles on how to embrace all your emotions and that sometimes you must accept how things really helped to raise my spiritual awareness and how to apply it to my everyday life.

*"Growth is painful. Change is painful. But, nothing as a painful as staying stuck where you don't belong"*
**N.R.Narayana Murthy**

## Acknowledgements

To my wife Louise, my two sons Oliver and Marcus, thank you for being the constant I need in my life to enable me to indulge myself on these journeys of discovery I take. Knowing that I have your unconditional love and support means more than I often express.

To the incredible people below without whom this book wouldn't exist, your willingness to give your time and counsel freely has been truly appreciated. I'll do my best to repay you in kind or at least wine and beer.

Mark Henderson, Director and Co-Owner of Bistro Live without your business savvy and support The Change Partner wouldn't look and feel like it does today.

Neil Lewis Founder at The Empathy Coach, my empathy guru, spiritual support and Thursday morning buddy without our regular chat's my self-confidence wouldn't be as unwavering as it is.

Darren Jones, my friend and gig companion for over 20 years, Independent HR Consultant and Founder of Instinct HR, without an innocent comment on his podcast this book wouldn't exist.

My brother Robin (Our Kid), thank you for our chats on change and leadership methodologies and on all thing's family, football and cycling. I'm also sorry for waking you up when you were younger by eating cornflakes after many a night out.

Andy Gibney and his talented team at 3P Publishing for helping me craft, edit and ultimately publish the book you're holding in your hands. Your expertise and experience proved invaluable.

To all the other people too numerous to mention that I've worked with, collaborated with, and chewed the fat with, thanks for your wise words, guidance, and patience to provide the lessons I've learned during my career to date. I've learnt from each and every one of you, much of which will stick with me forever.

*"The secret of change is to focus all of your energy not on fighting the old, but on building the new"*
*Socrates*

## About The Author

**Simon Costigan** was born in Preston, Lancashire, and currently lives in Derby, UK. He spent a large part of his career working for Boots UK and Walgreens, the global health and wellbeing business, where he learnt the fundamental skills of leading global change projects and programmes. Having the opportunity to work in a global blue-chip organisation enabled him to understand what best-in-class execution looked like, managing a global portfolio of over $500 million and delivering some of the world's most recognised products, such as the No7 serum ranges for women.

Having felt that his journey in the corporate world had run its course, he founded The Change Partner in 2020 (www.thechangepartner.co.uk), a consultancy that supports business of all sizes to deliver long-term, sustainable change initiatives through effective strategy planning, structured governance and reporting, and market-leading leadership development coaching and mentoring. Simon is married to Louise with two sons Oliver and Marcus and a Cockapoo called Teddy. He can be contacted at: simon@thechangepartner.co.uk

*"Change is much more than the coins you'll find in your pocket"*
*Simon Costigan*